Making
Garden
Furniture
From Wood

Making
Garden
Furniture
From Wood

Anthony Hontoir

The Crowood Press

First published in 2005 by
The Crowood Press Ltd
Ramsbury, Marlborough
Wiltshire SN8 2HR

www.crowood.com

British Library Cataloguing-in-Publication Data
A catalogue record for this book is available from the British
Library.

ISBN 1 86126 599 9

Designed and typeset by Focus Publishing, 11a St Botolph's
Road, Sevenoaks, Kent TN13 3AJ

Printed and bound in Malaysia by Times Offset (M) Sdn Bhd

Contents

Introduction

For many people, the garden is an extension of their home, regardless of its size and whether or not it is made up of beautifully maintained lawns and lovingly nurtured flower borders, or is simply a small patch of ground with a patio. Indeed, those of us who live in town houses with no garden at all can still create an outdoor atmosphere by using window ledges and balconies with a little imagination.

The garden gives us all an opportunity to enjoy outdoor life through the entire year, starting with the freshness of spring when new growth is just beginning to stir and come to life; the warmth of summer with its long hours of daylight and the opportunity this affords to eat outside; the coming of autumn, when fruit trees bear their annual crop; followed by the short cold days of winter, when we gaze out upon leafless branches and empty borders, knowing that it is time to help our small feathered garden visitors through the difficult months by offering them shelter in the form of birdhouses with the chance to provide sustenance. Each season brings its own view of nature, and the garden is our private version of it.

Like the home, no garden is complete unless it is provided with the right sort of furniture to suit our particular taste. For no matter how big or small the garden happens to be, whether we prefer to look out upon a broad expanse of green lawn, the myriad colours and mingled fragrances of planted flowerbeds, or trees and hedgerows in full blossom, our enjoyment of these wonderful outdoor surroundings is made so much more pleasurable when the garden or terrace is furnished with tables, chairs and the many other accessories that help to make it complete.

This book concerns itself with the building of traditional garden furniture, those items that we would consider essential for our comfort and convenience, in a traditionally accepted appearance or design. None of these items is either expensive or complicated to make: indeed, the woodworking techniques have been simplified throughout, to ensure that the reader does not require a great deal of knowledge and experience of woodwork. Nor should it be assumed that the workbench needs to be equipped with a vast array of costly and complex tools – in fact, rather to the contrary: the workbench for these projects does not need to be stocked with anything other than a set of basic, good quality woodworking tools. If you happen to be in possession of power tools and know how to use them safely and effectively, all well and good, but they are not a necessity to the achieving of first class results. There is always something particularly satisfying about producing a completed piece of woodwork entirely by hand, using a modest array of tools.

As for the reader's own individual ability, the usual advice is that it is wisest to commence with the easier items and progress gradually to the more difficult. However, joints and techniques have been kept as straightforward as possible, so even the larger projects are well within the scope of the reasonably competent woodworker. For the novice, it might seem rather daunting to contemplate making the bench seat, which is the biggest piece of furniture in the book, especially since it involves large sections of wood which may be quite expensive to purchase. But if you practise first on cutting the required joints – inevitably mortise and tenon joints – in small sections of the same wood and follow the old axiom of 'measure twice and cut once', you will probably surprise yourself with the way you quickly progress.

Before describing in easy step-by-step instructions how each of the projects is made, the first chapters set out the basis of our approach to tools and materials, and the joints that are most commonly employed throughout the book. Each of the projects has a high degree of versatility, in that the design can be adapted or modified to suit the size of the garden for which it is intended, or to create an object that will serve a different purpose.

Where you have the greatest choice in any matter, is in the type of finish that is applied to the wood when the piece of furniture has been completed. These days there are so many different types of wood finish available that it is very hard to decide which is best, although to some extent the question is simplified by the fact that all of the items are intended for outdoor use, with one or two exceptions which could be considered more suitable for the conservatory, and therefore mostly you will need to opt for a water-resistant finish which will protect the wood from long periods of exposure to sun, wind and rain. It is then more a matter of determining the colour of the finish and judging the surface appearance of the wood after it has been applied and allowed to dry thoroughly: both of these being considerations of personal preference.

The best advice with regard to the treatment of the wood is to use offcuts and experiment with a variety of finishes until you obtain the result you find most satisfactory; and of course a more expensive product should give you better and longer-lasting protection.

No more need be said by way of introduction, other than to wish you the best of luck with your endeavours in the hope that the designs in the following pages will enhance your own garden, patio, terrace, conservatory or whatever provides you with your access to the outdoor world.

CHAPTER 1

Tools and Materials

It is possible to make most of the items in this book without needing a fully equipped workshop, although the more facilities and tools that are available to you, the easier it will be to produce good quality results. With a little ingenuity, a handful of basic tools, and some space at one end of the kitchen table, there is no reason why the keen woodworker cannot make pieces of furniture to the highest standard of finish. On the other hand, this is not really the most satisfactory way of proceeding, for several reasons.

A proper working area is recommended, whether it is a spare room inside the house, part of the garage or a garden shed. Timber tends to be supplied in long lengths, and you require space in order to handle it safely and efficiently. A workbench of some sort is essential, whether it is a purpose-made wooden bench equipped with a vice, a fold-away version or merely a sturdy table to which you can clamp the material whilst you work on it. The area needs to be dry, with reasonable ventilation, and preferably supplied with electricity for the provision of adequate lighting and to power any special tools that you may happen to own.

The working area should also be kept *clean*. This is particularly important from a safety point of view. Accumulated off-cuts of wood, shavings and sawdust build up very quickly, and present a fire hazard. Waste material should be gathered up at the end of every session and placed in rubbish bags for disposal. Apart from anything else, an untidy workshop is more likely to encourage accidents, and safety should *always* be uppermost in your mind.

Even the most harmless-looking tools can be dangerous, if stored or handled incorrectly. Sharp chisels should always have their tips covered when not in use, and manipulated with the greatest of care; saws should be hung up in a special place when not needed; and power tools demand constant vigilance. You are most likely to own an electric drill, planer, jigsaw and possibly a router if you have any power tools at all, and each of these can do great damage in a fraction of a second.

None of this is intended to put you off! Indeed, woodwork is a wonderful pastime, for you can see the results of all your hard effort taking shape in front of you, and often it gives you the opportunity to make something that it is not *quite* possible to go out and buy, or something that you could not afford to buy, and you have the personal satisfaction of knowing that the job is well done.

TOOLS

Whether you are a newcomer to woodwork, with only a limited set of basic hand tools, or an experienced practitioner with a fully stocked toolbox, it is the purpose of this book to show you how a range of useful and attractive items for the garden can be built without the need for a large array of complicated and expensive tools. For those who already possess a well equipped workshop full of power tools, it clearly makes sense to put these to full use, but this does not mean that you cannot achieve excellent results without them.

There are, naturally, a number of tools that must be considered essential if you are to produce top quality results. If you do not already own any of these, you must be prepared to purchase most, if not all, of the hand tools listed below. The power tools are desirable – though not essential – but you will find that many DIY stores have a range of these tools that are not exceptionally expensive and could prove a worthwhile investment, provided you take care with them. Let us consider the types of tool that you should aim to include in your tool cabinet.

Tape Measure

All woodwork depends on accurate measurement, and the rule or tape measure is probably used more than any other tool. My own choice is the spring-loaded flexible steel tape measure that pulls out from a plastic or metal casing, has a lock to hold it in any position, and retracts back into the casing when not in use. The scale is usually marked in inches and centimetres. An L-shaped steel lip is attached to the free end of the tape, and serves to mark the zero position. When the tape is calibrated in both imperial and metric measurements, always take care not to mix them up. For example, it is never a good idea to start working in inches and then convert to millimetres in the middle of a project, as there will always be a slight difference in the conversion process. Although there is a legal requirement to sell material in metric measurements, many people still prefer to work in inches. All measurements are quoted in millimetres and inches in this book, but for practical purposes metric figures should take precedence for the sake of accuracy.

Pencil

It is hard to think of the everyday pencil as being a tool, but it has a very important role to play in woodwork, for everything that needs to be cut or joined also needs to be marked. I normally use an ordinary HB pencil that I keep well sharpened to retain a fine point. Do not use a pencil with a hard lead, because this will score the surface of the wood, and a very soft lead will quickly lose its ability to draw a thin line. An HB lead is a good compromise.

Marking Knife

This is used to mark a thin line on the surface of the wood, as in the case of going over the previously squared pencil line of a tenon, so that the teeth of the saw, when cutting on the waste side of the line, do not rip the grain beyond the line and disfigure the wood.

Square

In the process of marking the wood for cutting and jointing, it is the usual practice to draw a line at right-angles to its length. The try-square consists of a rectangular wooden handle, edged in brass, that has a steel blade attached to it at 90 degrees with two parallel edges. A more sophisticated version of the plain try-square is the mitre square, whose adjustable blade can be set at any angle between 45 degrees and 90 degrees.

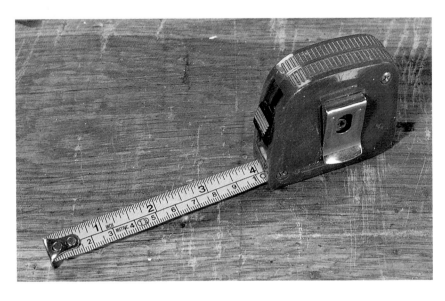

A retractable steel tape measure.

*The mortise gauge,
which also serves as a
marking gauge.*

Mortise Gauge

This tool is used to scribe two parallel lines along a piece of wood for the marking out of the mortise and tenon joint, for instance, and it has two spurs, one of which is fixed, the other being adjustable, so that the gap between the two parallel lines may be set as required. The best types of mortise gauge are equipped with a rounded brass thumbscrew at the opposite end from the spurs, to control the position of the inner movable spur with great precision. The sliding wooden fence, which is released and tightened by means of a screw, can be locked in any position, and provides the means of guiding the gauge along the length of the wood that it is scribing. Most mortise gauges combine two functions by having the double spurs for the marking of mortises and suchlike, but when needed, the adjustable spur can be tucked into the fence to leave only the fixed spur for single line marking.

Tenon Saw

As its name implies, the tenon saw is used for cutting tenons and other types of joint where fine sawing is required. It is quite a short saw, and has between twelve and twenty teeth to the inch. The top edge of the blade is strengthened with a steel or brass back to give rigidity and ensure a straight cut, and for this reason it is also known as the backsaw. The blade length ranges from 200mm (8in) to 305mm (12in). A firm wooden handgrip is an advantage.

Handsaw

This is a general-purpose saw that you will use to do most of your preparatory, or rough, cutting. It normally measures around 610mm (24in) in length, and

has either eight or ten teeth to the inch. The teeth are set in an alternating pattern – as they are with the tenon saw, except here it is more pronounced – so that as the saw cuts into the wood it creates a passage known as the kerf, which is wider than the thickness of the blade, thus ensuring that the saw does not bind or jam as it passes through the wood. The handsaw does not have a strengthened back, so it is flexible, and the manipulation of this type of saw requires some skill to maintain a perfectly straight cut.

Coping Saw

This is a very useful saw when you need to cut curves. The thin blade is mounted in a metal frame shaped in the form of a U, and held under tension by tightening the handgrip. If the handgrip is slackened off, the blade can be rotated about its axis within the frame to set it at any desired angle. The extent to which it can cut the wood, however, is always determined by the saw's frame.

Electric Jigsaw

In its most common form, this is a hand-held power tool in which the saw blade oscillates up and down at very high speed to provide a fast and highly manoeuvrable means of cutting. Various blades may be fitted, ranging from fine to coarse. The more expensive models of jigsaw have a variable-speed cutting action, governed by the amount of finger pressure exerted on the switch.

Chisel

It is advisable to have a set of good quality chisels covering a range of sizes so that you can select the most suitable width of blade for the job in hand. Typical

A bevelled chisel.

blade widths would be 6mm (¼in), 9mm (⅜in), 13mm (½in), 16mm (⅝in), 19mm (¾in) and 25mm (1in). The firmer chisel has a strong cutting blade with square edges, whereas the bevelled chisel has two sloped edges, making the tool ideal for cutting dovetail joints, although dovetails do not appear in any of the projects in this book.

Mallet

A large wooden hammer, intended for striking the chisel in chopping out joints, and for knocking together the various pieces of wood that make up an assembly. The mallet should *not* be used for driving in nails, a task that must be left to a conventional steel hammer.

Smoothing Plane

This is the most frequently used bench plane. It is made from steel, and is fitted with a wooden or plastic handle and knob. The cutting blade is easily detachable for sharpening and adjusting the depth of the cut.

Electric Plane

This is a high-speed tool that does much the same work as the smoothing plane, except that the physical effort is reduced and the task of planing down the wood made a lot quicker. The planing action is facilitated by a revolving drum that carries two identical blades placed 180 degrees apart. As the drum spins at speeds of up to 20,000rpm, the blades alternately come into contact with the surface of the wood and remove small amounts as the plane is pushed forward. There is a knob for altering the depth of the cut,

which works by raising or lowering the sole at the front, whilst the position of the spinning drum remains constant. With prolonged use, the rubber drive belt has a tendency to snap, and occasionally needs replacing with a new one, but this is an easy task.

Spokeshave

The function of the spokeshave is mainly to shape curved surfaces, and it is an invaluable tool for dealing with sweeping curves, such as those encountered on the arms and legs of chairs. It may not be called into use very often, but is an excellent tool when required.

Handbrace

This tool is used for the majority of drilling operations. It consists of a crank forged from steel, which is fitted with a rounded wooden or plastic handle at one end and a chuck at the other, for holding a variety of drill bits, ranging from small twist drills, auger bits and centre bits.

Pillar Drill

This is a very useful piece of workshop equipment, for it combines the speed and convenience of an electric drill with the precision of being held in a vertical stand. The drill may have a variety of speeds, determined by a series of pulleys and drive belts that are easily adjustable, and the drilling action is controlled by a spring-loaded up-and-down movement. This machine, which needs to be bolted very securely to a strong worktop, is excellent for boring out the first stage of waste when preparing mortises.

Electric Router

There is always an element of mystery about a tool that has a reputation for performing many tasks, such as rebating, grooving, fluting and edge-moulding, but in fact the electric router is simply a motor housed vertically inside the body of the tool, which drives a chuck at very high revolutions. Into the chuck may be fitted a wide range of cutters, although its use in this book is confined to the preparation of rebates and housing grooves. The base of the router is circular, so that it can be lined up against a length of straight-edged batten, acting as a guide, and steered through any angle without deviating from a straight path. A detachable fence can be mounted beneath the base to provide the router with its own adjustable guide, and the spring-loaded plunging action of the body may be pre-set against a scaled depth-stop so that the cutter is accurately controlled both laterally and vertically.

CARING FOR TOOLS

The most effective way of looking after all your wood-working tools is to store them away safely when they are not in use, rather than leave them lying around on the worktop. If your workplace is in the garage or garden shed where the atmosphere is likely to be damp, you can safeguard all steel surfaces from rust by giving them a regular rub over with a soft cloth soaked in light oil.

Inspect saw blades, chisels and planes regularly to ensure that their cutting edges are always keen and efficient. An oilstone is an absolute must for periodically re-sharpening chisels and planes. Remember also that many tools are designed to cut wood, and they are none too particular about cutting careless fingers as well. Power tools are especially dangerous in this respect, and require careful handling at all times. Learn how to hold and manipulate these tools properly, and stay safe at all times.

MATERIALS

Before you can begin making any piece of garden furniture, you must decide what sort of wood you are going to use. The decision is not as difficult as would be the case for many other kinds of woodwork,

because by its nature, garden furniture often calls for a material that is basic and will withstand outdoor conditions. Nothing delicate or exquisite is demanded here. Most of the items in this book are made from either the sort of softwood that you can buy from any timber merchant or DIY store, or one or two hardwoods that are not difficult to obtain, such as sapele, utile and iroko.

The terms 'softwood' and 'hardwood' can be misleading, for the names suggest that hardwoods are tough and durable, whilst softwoods are weaker and more susceptible to breakage. In fact, certain hardwoods are relatively soft, and a few of the softwoods are particularly hard, so clearly the generic name is misleading, for it does not refer to the actual hardness or softness of the material. However, it so happens in this case that whitewood or redwood, which are typically the softwoods that you might expect to find on the shelf at your nearest timber stockist, are in fact quite soft, and iroko is especially hard and unyielding, although it produces very good results.

Unless you wish to purchase more exotic or expensive materials, such as parana pine, oak, maple or walnut for your own garden, you would be advised to keep to the types of wood that are most readily available and not too expensive.

How Timber Is Supplied

Whether you intend to buy your wood from the timber merchant, the DIY store or some other outlet, possibly a garden centre that has a few sizes of wood for sale, it is supplied in two forms: sawn or planed. When cut from the log and subsequently sawn into smaller sections, the surface of the wood is rather coarse, although it may be considered ideal for certain kinds of outdoor woodwork, such as fencing. The main characteristic of sawn wood is its dimensions, for if a particular piece is quoted as being 50×25mm (2×1in) in cross-section, that is exactly what it should measure.

Planed wood, also known by the initials PSE (planed square edge) or PAR (planed all round), in contrast to sawn wood, has its sides and edges prepared from the roughly sawn state by passing it through a planing machine, which skims off some of the surface to leave a smooth finish. To obtain this result, there must clearly be some reduction in the dimensions of the material, equal to the amount taken off by the plane. Prepared wood is therefore fractionally smaller in cross-section than its sawn equivalent, and there are two ways in which it may be quoted. For example, the same 50 × 25mm (2 × 1in) piece in the planed form can be referred to as either 50 × 25mm (2 × 1in) prepared, or 45 × 19mm (1¾ × ¾in) finished size, PSE or PAR.

There should be no problem in obtaining any amount of softwood from the timber merchant in a range of standard sizes, but hardwoods can present more difficulties. You will either have to choose from the limited varieties that are held in stock, or place a special order. If you have a local joinery that specializes in making doors and windows, it may be worth asking if they have off-cuts or lengths of hardwood left over from a particular job; and even if they do not have exactly what you want in stock, they will probably have the means to get it for you.

Faults In Wood

The fact that wood is being offered for sale does not necessarily mean that it is in perfect condition, and there are several faults that you should look out for. If you are buying a softwood such as pine or deal, the most obvious characteristic is the knot. This is the point at which a branch joined the trunk of the tree. Provided the knot is live and quite small, it should present no real problem, but large dead knots are a liability and ought to be avoided. They are distinguished by a surrounding black mark, and often the centre of the knot is ready to fall out, if it has not already done so.

Knotty wood is quite acceptable for garden furniture, and besides, when you give it a thorough application of wood preservative and finish, which often contains a colour, by the time you have finished treating the wood, the knots are hardly noticeable. Even so, you should still be selective when you buy your wood, and only take the best lengths available.

A badly warped board is not much use to the woodworker – unless you want it like that for a reason, or can cut it up into narrower sections and plane the warp out. The distortion is caused by uneven drying of the sap in the wood. Another bad fault is known as 'shakes', which are splits or cracks running through a length of timber, rendering it virtually useless.

Take care when you buy your wood. Decide whether it is to be softwood or hardwood, and if necessary, obtain a quotation from your timber supplier to make sure that they will give you good value for money.

Knots such as this one are hard to avoid in softwoods such as pine.

CHAPTER 2

Jointing Techniques

The joints used in the making of garden furniture are of a somewhat more basic nature than those generally employed in the construction of household furniture and joinery, for the items themselves are often less elaborate or complicated, and the jointing is, quite commonly, of a heavier kind in order to cope with outdoor conditions.

At its simplest, a joint consists of nothing more than placing one piece of wood against another and knocking them both together with a couple of nails. This is a butt joint, and is the sort of straightforward method that you would use if you were building a garden fence, for instance, where horizontal crosspieces are attached to upright posts, and the fencing sections applied vertically to the crosspieces. Apart from the need for a tape measure, spirit level and hammer, little more is required, and yet the resulting fence, with care, will look neat and practical and, if cared for with regular applications of wood preservative, should last for years.

At its most complicated, a piece of garden furniture such as a bench seat needs the same type of jointing as an interior chair, except that the wood sections will undoubtedly be larger, the finished article heavier, and the conditions under which it has to survive from day to day more extreme. In this case, the mortise and tenon joint is used.

In between these two examples we will be using mitre joints, dowel joints, halved joints and housing joints, but little else besides. If you already have a thorough knowledge of how these joints function, and the methods used to make them, you can safely pass on to the next chapter. If, on the other hand, woodwork is a new subject to you and you simply

wish to make something useful for your garden, read on: you already know, from what has been said in the last chapter, that you need a reasonable selection of good quality tools. Now you can find out how they are applied to make the joints that will be needed in the projects that lie ahead.

BUTT JOINT

The butt joint is formed when the edges or sides of two pieces of wood are brought together, or the edge of one piece and the side of the other. Usually the wood is planed and has square corners, and indeed, all of the timber used in the ensuing projects is of this variety. However, certain types of garden furniture

The butt joint.

The mitre joint.

have a more rustic appearance, and you may choose to make some of the following items from roughly sawn timber. In either case, the nature of the joint remains the same.

The main point in its favour is the ease with which it can be made. Being a surface joint, in which two flat surfaces or edges are butted up against each other, the abutment between the two parts only allows for the joint to be laid in position. There are various ways of making the joint secure: it can be assembled with strong wood glue, nails or screws, or glue and dowels.

Preparation of the butt joint is limited to cutting the wood to size and, usually, ensuring that the surfaces are planed smooth and flat, and thus able to make complete contact with each other.

MITRE JOINT

The mitre joint is normally formed by two pieces of wood having their ends cut at an angle of 45 degrees so they meet to form a right-angled corner. In certain types of work the angle may be varied to a larger or smaller angle, but the 90-degree mitre joint remains the most common, and some of the mitres in this book are created from a single piece of wood being mitred at 45 degrees and butted up against another to form a simple support. The mitre may be assembled with glue, but this alone does not provide enough strength, and it is usual to reinforce the joint with nails.

There are two ways of preparing the simple mitre,

which consists of no more than one or two lengths of wood with a 45-degree angle cut at one end. The first method is to measure out the position where the angled cut is to be made on the piece of wood, and mark across it with the mitre square, which has its blade set at an angle of 45 degrees. Square at right angles across the two edges, and repeat the 45-degree angle on the opposite side, always working from face side and face edge. Clamp the piece to the workbench or hold it in the bench hook, and cut off the waste with the tenon saw. The angled cut can then be trimmed by placing the wood on a mitre shooting board and planing it smooth.

The second method starts in the same way, by measuring the position of the joint on both lengths of wood, but instead of marking with the mitre square, the piece is cut by placing it in a mitre box, lining it up in the appropriate position with the 45-degree saw guides, and cutting away the waste with the tenon saw. In either instance, you rely for accuracy on the use of a special jig – the shooting board or the mitre box. Both of these can be bought, or you can make your own.

Dowel Joint

The dowel joint can take several forms, but in general it is similar to the butt joint except that it is precisely located and fastened by one or more lengths of wooden dowelling. The purpose of the dowel, or peg, is to serve as a fixing pin, which is glued to both parts of the joint and thus locates them permanently in place. It has two important functions: first, it holds the joint firm against any tendency to pull apart; and second, it prevents the two joining surfaces from sliding laterally.

Since the dowels serve to reinforce what amounts to a simple butt joint, the overall effect is to secure the two pieces of wood doubly, with the butt joint taking effect by having glue applied along its entire joining surfaces. The dowel joint, therefore, offers potential for great strength. If the dowels only were to be glued, then the strength of the resulting joint would depend merely on the cross-sectional area of the dowels, which is small compared with the joint's total area.

The dowel joint is often regarded as one of the more recent innovations in woodwork, acting as a substitute for the mortise and tenon joint in many contemporary designs, but it does have a long history of use, dating back to some of the earliest types of furniture. Dowels are also used to provide decoration in the form of rails, and these are simply glued into receiver holes, usually of the stopped variety, which means that they do not pass right through the wood but are drilled to a pre-determined depth.

Dowelling is sold commercially in long lengths covering a range of standard diameters, and is usually made from the light-coloured hardwood called ramin. The most common sizes are 6mm (¼in), 9mm (⅜in), 13mm (½in), 16mm (⅝in) and 19mm (¾in). Occasionally you may find a slight discrepancy between the diameter of the dowel material and the drill bit used to bore out the receiver holes, giving you a dowel that is either too loose in its hole or too big to fit. For this reason it makes sense to carry out a trial run on a piece of scrap wood before you begin preparing your dowel joints in the workpiece. Ideally, the dowel should slide into its hole with no more than firm pressure from the fingers.

There are two distinct types of dowel joint used in this book. The first of these is the dowel that is used to pin two pieces of wood that have already been butt-jointed together. The second type is the dowel joint that serves as an alternative to the mortise and tenon joint, joining the end grain of one piece to the edge or side of another, as in the construction of a chair frame.

Taking the first example, the dowelling method is quite straightforward. One piece of wood is directly butt-jointed to another, or set into a housing groove, and glued in place, and to make the joint more secure, a hole is bored through both the joining pieces and a length of dowel glued into this hole instead of fasten-

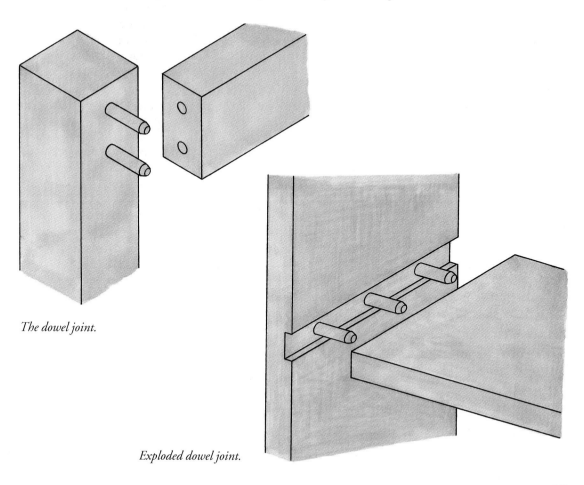

The dowel joint.

Exploded dowel joint.

ing with nails or screws. It is used to fix table-top slats to the frame, for instance. In the second example, a dowel joint is formed between the edge of a chair leg and the end grain of a rail. Two dowels are normally employed in order to resist any turning movement, although if the wood is small in size only one dowel may sometimes be accommodated.

Mark and cut out a card template equal in size to the cross-sectional dimensions of the rail, as represented by the end grain. Measure and draw a line along the centre of the template, and then set in the dowel positions. In deciding how near to the edges the dowels should be, as a rough guide you can divide the length of the template – that is, the depth of the rail – into four parts, and mark the dowels at the first and third intersections with the centre line.

When preparing to mark the dowel positions on the side or edge of the leg, it is a wise precaution to measure the leg so that it is slightly longer than necessary. In this way you avoid placing the template with

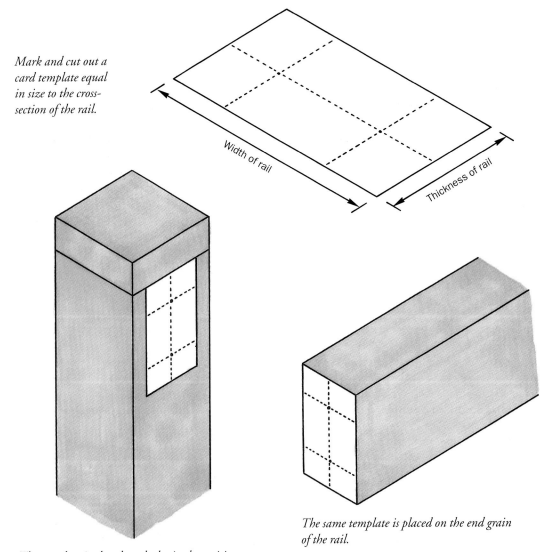

Mark and cut out a card template equal in size to the cross-section of the rail.

Width of rail

Thickness of rail

The same template is placed on the end grain of the rail.

The template is placed on the leg in the position to be occupied by the rail.

18

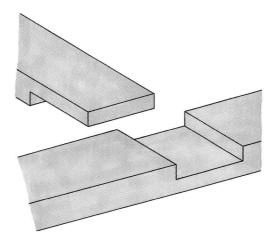

The halved joint.

its top edge lying flush with the end of the wood, and thus reduce the risk of the wood splitting when the top dowel hole is drilled. The same template is then carefully placed on the end grain of the rail, which has already been cut perfectly square, and the dowel hole positions marked in each case. It is not always as easy to make a clear mark on end grain in pencil, as would be the case for marking on the side or edge of the leg, so it is probably better to make the mark with a bradawl.

All the dowel holes must be drilled with great precision. This is easily achieved with the holes in the leg by mounting the wood on a pillar drill. However, it is often rather difficult, when drilling into end grain, to prevent the drill bit from wandering off the mark, owing to the fibrous nature of the wood grain when approached end on. Some of the denser woods present little cause for concern, and the auger bit makes a smooth, straight passage into the wood. For the looser-grained woods, it would be advisable to use a dowel jig for absolute precision. The depth to which the dowel holes are drilled clearly depends on the size of the wood.

When the dowels are cut to length from the dowelling material, they should be slightly less than the combined depth of the dowel holes, and it is a good idea to bevel their ends slightly by giving a few twists in a pencil sharpener, and possibly to run the blade of the tenon saw along the length of the dowel so that the shallow kerf provides a glue passage along which any excess wood glue can escape during the assembling of the joint.

HALVED JOINT

The halved joint, or lapped joint as it is also known, is used to join together two lengths of wood, usually at right angles, by removing half the thickness from both pieces so that when they are brought into contact their surfaces remain flush. The joint can either be located along the length of the wood, or at the end of it.

There are several possible variations to this joint, the most common being where the two pieces of wood that are being joined together are of different thicknesses, and occasionally it consists of little more than a shallow notch being cut in the wood to provide a means of accurately locating the butting together of two pieces. The preparation of the joint consists of accurately measuring the width of one piece of wood, and transferring this measurement on to the surface or edge of the other, squaring pencil lines across to mark in its position, and then setting the pointer of a marking gauge to the required depth of the joint and scribing a line along each edge.

Remove the waste by making a series of saw-cuts on the marked-out area with the tenon saw, cutting down *just* to the scribed depth line, and then chopping away the waste with a broad-bladed chisel and mallet, working the chisel blade firstly from one edge and then from the other, in order to prevent the wood from splitting away beyond the waste line. Clean away any surplus strands of waste with the sharp tip of the chisel blade, and finally assemble the joint with wood glue, applying the glue thoroughly to the joining surfaces.

HOUSING JOINT

The housing joint is formed by fitting the end of one piece of wood into a groove cut along the length, or across the grain, of the second piece, so that when the two parts are brought together they result in a recessed right-angled joint.

The simplest type of housing joint consists of a groove whose width is equal to the thickness of the wood that fits into it. The groove runs along the length of the piece in which it is cut. It is prepared by measuring the thickness of the piece that is to be housed inside the groove, and setting the two spurs of a mortise gauge to this amount, and adjusting the fence of the gauge so that two parallel lines may be scribed in the required position along one edge of the piece that is to be grooved. The simplest way of preparing the groove is to cut it out with the electric router, fitted with a straight-edged bit equal in width to the groove, and setting the depth of the router to the desired depth of the groove.

Clamp the wood to the edge of the workbench, or hold it securely in the vice, and make several passes with the router, commencing with a shallow cut, and increasing it until the spring-loaded plunging action reaches the depth-stop that you have set on it.

MORTISE AND TENON JOINT

This is one of the most common and important joints in woodwork. It consists of a mortise, or opening, cut into one piece of wood, and a tenon, or tongue, equal in size to the mortise, cut at the end of the second piece. It possesses great potential strength, can be adapted to a wide variety of uses, and in the majority of cases, remains well concealed inside the wood. Its strength lies in the fact that the joining surfaces cover a relatively large area over which the wood glue can act.

There are a number of variations to this versatile joint. For example, some tenons are cut with two shoulders, while others are more refined with four. Those that have only one main shoulder are known as 'bare-faced' tenons. Some mortises pass right through the wood to come out on the opposite side or edge, called 'through mortises'. Others stop short within the wood and are not visible from outside; these are called 'stopped mortises'. There are also the haunched tenon, and the mitred tenon.

For greatest strength, the assembled joints are held firm with dowel pegs. When pegs are fitted, the hole in the tenon is usually off-set slightly from the

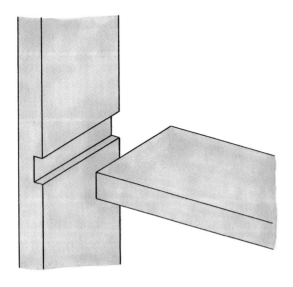

The housing joint.

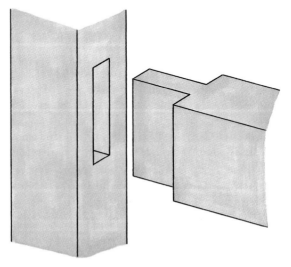

The mortise and tenon joint.

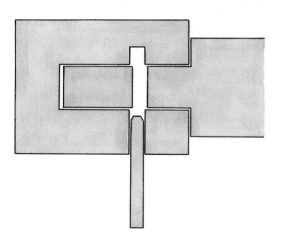

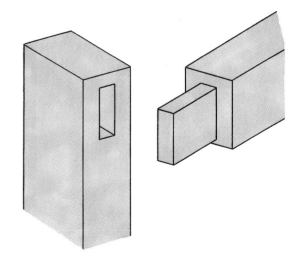

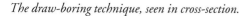

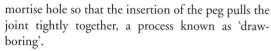

The draw-boring technique, seen in cross-section.

The four-shouldered stopped mortise and tenon joint.

mortise hole so that the insertion of the peg pulls the joint tightly together, a process known as 'draw-boring'.

The mortise and tenon joint occurs in such a wide variety of circumstances that it is virtually impossible to say that any one situation is typical. Having said that, as far as the projects in this book are concerned, it may be stated that the requirement here is mostly for two-shouldered or four-shouldered stopped mortise and tenon joints.

The theory of the mortise and tenon joint is that the mortise, and therefore the tenon, should be equal to one-third the thickness of the wood in which they are cut. This holds up perfectly well when both parts of the joint are prepared from pieces of the same thickness, but it often happens that the design requires that one piece should be thicker than the other: the leg of a table or chair is normally of a greater thickness than the rail. It is usual to arrange for the mortise and tenon to be as wide as possible, so the one-third rule is applied to the greater thickness, which is the leg. Assuming that the rail is not less than one-third the leg thickness, a tenon can still be cut successfully, even though it has shallower shoulders.

For simplicity, in the following description of how to make the joint, let us assume that the mortise and tenon are to be cut from pieces of equal width and thickness. First, check that the sides and edges are all planed straight and square. Even when the wood has

been supplied by the local timber merchant to your own specified dimensions, it is still wise to run the tape measure over each individual piece to ensure that it is of the required width and thickness.

Start by marking in the position of the mortise. When it is to be set close to the end of the wood, as when joining a seat rail to a front chair leg, allow at least 25mm (1in) extra to serve as a safety margin, so that when the mortise is being cut there is sufficient wood to prevent the piece from splitting. After the mortise has been cut, and before the joint is fitted together, this surplus is trimmed. There is no need to allow a safety margin for a mortise placed along the length of the wood, because enough material exists at both ends of the joint.

Mark out with the tape measure, square and pencil. Measure the distance from the end of the wood and square two lines across the edge of the piece where you want to make the mortise, separating the lines by an amount equal to the width of the rail in which the tenon will be cut.

Set the distance between the two spurs of a mortise gauge to the width of the chisel that is nearest in size to one-third the thickness of the wood, and adjust the fence of the gauge until the two spurs make a pair of tiny impressions centrally on the edge. You can easily check whether or not the two points are dead centre by holding the fence against each of the opposing sides in turn: when the impressions coincide from

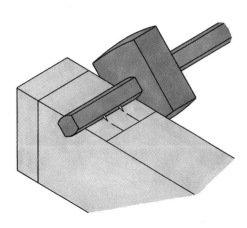

Mark a pair of parallel lines with the mortise gauge between the two squared pencil lines.

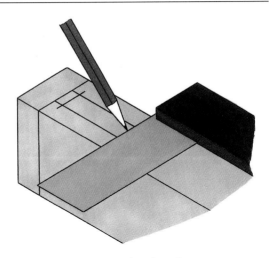

The mortise is inset at each end, so that it is entirely concealed from view in the finished joint.

both directions, you know that you are precisely in the middle. Even so, it is still advisable to work the gauge from the face side for all marking operations. Run the gauge along the edge of the wood so that the two spurs inscribe a pair of parallel lines between the two squared pencil lines.

If the tenon is to have four shoulders, which is preferable although not essential, the next task is to measure and mark the setting in of the mortise at each end. These amounts depend on where the mortise is situated. For example, when the mortise is positioned very near to the end of the wood, the distance must be sufficient to prevent the end grain from breaking away when the tenon is fitted. But the other end of the mortise needs only a small setting in, just enough to prevent the tenon from being visible when the joint is assembled. If the mortise is to be placed along the length of the wood, far removed from either end grain, it only needs to be set in by a small amount at both ends.

Decide how much of an inset you require, and measure this distance at the two ends of the mortise with the tape measure, marking with the pencil and squaring across the edge of the piece. The mortise has now assumed the shape of a clearly defined box, bounded by a pair of inscribed lines from the mortise gauge and squared pencil lines.

One further point to consider is how far down into the wood the mortise should be cut. The generally

accepted rule for a stopped mortise is that it should be equal in depth to three-quarters the width of the piece in which it is cut, although this is a somewhat arbitrary figure. Also, chair legs have mortises cut in adjacent sides, to accommodate the seat rails, and these often meet within the wood.

Although it is perfectly feasible to remove all the waste from the mortise with the chisel and mallet, this is an unnecessarily long drawn-out task. To speed up the process, much of the waste may be drilled out by boring a series of holes along the length of the mortise. It is important that the drill bit should be slightly smaller in diameter than the width of the mortise, so that each drilled hole fits comfortably within the scribed lines. The pillar drill is an excellent tool for this purpose, since it is fitted with its own depth gauge to measure precisely the depth of each hole, and thus the mortise.

Chop out the remainder of the waste with the chisel and mallet. Starting near the centre, the first chisel cuts are made with the chisel inclined at an angle so that, when worked from both directions, the cutting forms a V-shape. As you progress deeper and further back towards the two ends of the mortise, you should gradually bring the chisel up to the vertical. Stop fractionally short of the two squared end lines, because as you prise out waste from the deepest part of the mortise, you will find that the levering action of the chisel makes a dent in the wood. Once the mortise has been almost completely chopped out, you may then place the chisel blade on each of the two end lines and, with the tool held absolutely vertical, strike hard with the mallet to make a final downward cut to complete the mortise.

To mark and cut out the tenon, begin by taking the measurement for the depth of the mortise, and transfer slightly less than this distance to the end of the piece in which the tenon is to be prepared. Square right around the wood at this point, working the

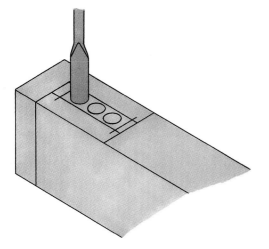

Most of the waste is removed from the mortise by drilling a series of holes along its length.

square from the face side and face edge. With the mortise gauge set as previously, scribe the two parallel lines along the two edges and the end grain of the wood, working the gauge from the face side for all three pairs of lines. Remember that if a rail is narrower than the leg, as is often the case in table and chair construction, the mortise gauge fence will need to be adjusted to centralize the lines for the tenon.

Clamp the wood in the workbench vice at an angle of approximately 45 degrees, and cut on the waste side of the marked lines with the tenon saw as far down as the squared shoulder line. Turn the piece around and repeat the same cut from the opposite edge. Finally, holding it in an upright position in the vice, saw straight down.

Remove the piece from the vice and, laying it flat on the workbench, place the square against each of the shoulder lines pencilled across the two sides of the wood, and score along both lines with the marking knife. Hold the piece firmly in the bench hook, or clamp it horizontally in the vice, and cut down on the waste side of the marked lines to remove the shoulders.

The next stage is to cut the third and fourth shoulders, where they are required, to match the setting in at both ends of the mortise. Place the rail in position with respect to the leg, and make pencil marks on the tenon to indicate where the two ends of the mortise

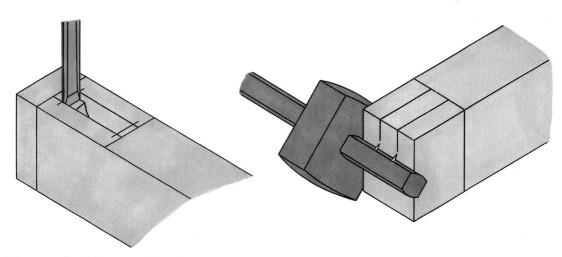

The remainder of the waste is chopped out from the mortise with the chisel.

The mortise gauge marks an identical pair of parallel lines for the tenon.

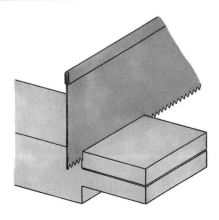

Cut off the two main portions of waste with the tenon saw.

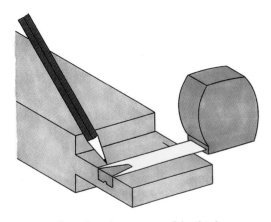

Measure and mark in the positions of the third and fourth shoulders to match the setting in at both ends of the mortise.

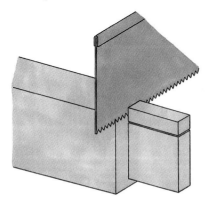

Complete the cutting of the third and fourth shoulders.

occur. Mark in these lines along the length of the tenon with the pencil and ruler. A special technique employed by experienced woodworkers is to grip the pencil so that the tips of your fingers press against the edge of the wood, and run your hand up and down the length of the tenon to make a straight line with the pencil's point.

Clamp the piece upright in the vice again, and saw down the lines as far as the main shoulder line; then re-position it horizontally, and complete cutting off the waste to create the second pair of shoulders.

The tenon should now fit fully into the mortise with only a light tapping of the mallet. If resistance is felt, remove the tenon from the mortise and, where you can see shiny marks on the cheeks of the tenon caused by the binding of the surfaces, gently pare off a few shavings of wood with the chisel, trimming until the tenon fits perfectly.

The stopped mortise and tenon joint is assembled with wood glue, the glue being applied to all the joining surfaces with a brush, and the two parts tapped together and cramped securely for the duration of the glue's drying time.

The pegging of a mortise and tenon joint is favoured for certain types of work. The dowel peg has been in use since the earliest days of woodwork, although with the advent of powerful synthetic wood glues, the need for the peg has somewhat diminished – but it still retains one important function: the process known as draw-boring.

In draw-boring, holes are bored through the sides of the mortise and tenon. This is done so that, with the hole in the tenon being slightly off-set from those in the mortise, when a dowel peg is driven in, it serves to draw the tenon further into the joint, and the result is a very secure fixture. A small or medium-sized joint will only require one peg, but a large joint will need two. The dowels may be 6mm (¼in) or 9mm (⅜in) in diameter, and their receiver holes are drilled with matching auger bits.

The positioning of the hole, or holes, is not critical, but you should aim for it to be somewhere near the centre of the tenon cheek for a single peg, or spaced regularly apart for two pegs, with plenty of tenon on either side. Once the position has been roughly determined on the tenon, it is a simple matter to transfer this by measurement to the side of the

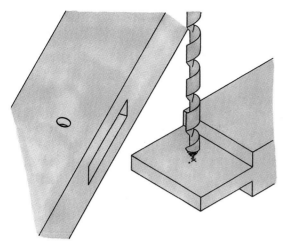

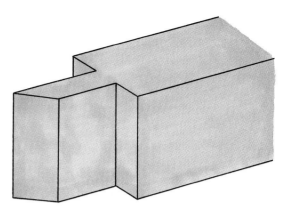

Draw-boring – drilling the offset hole though the tenon.

A mitred tenon.

mortise. Although the drilled hole must pass right through the mortise and into the wood on the other side, it must not be allowed to break through on the opposite surface of the wood. Fit the tenon into the mortise and mark the position of the hole, then remove the tenon again and set the position of the hole 2mm (³⁄₃₂in) nearer to the tenon's shoulder, drilling right through it.

Cut the dowel peg to length, and chamfer the end that is to be driven into the hole so that it has the ability to push its way into the off-set tenon without baulking, as would be the case if the end were left square. The pegged mortise and tenon joint is glued together, but due to the pulling effect of the draw-boring technique, there is no need to cramp up the assembly.

The mitred tenon is used when two rails are joined at right-angles to the same leg, so that the two stopped mortises combine with one another deep inside the wood. If each tenon were cut to fit its own mortise, a part of it would block the entry of the other – so the problem is resolved by cutting 45-degree mitre joints at the end of both tenons, enabling each one to fit fully into its own mortise without interfering with the other.

CHOICE OF WOOD GLUE

The most convenient wood glue is the sort that comes ready to use in a plastic bottle, known as the PVA variety. For the making of outdoor wooden items, particularly those that will be left out in all weather conditions, you should choose the waterproof type. You can also obtain wood glue in powdered resin form, which needs to be carefully measured out and mixed with a precise quantity of water to produce a usable mixture.

Although wood glue starts to set fairly quickly, it usually takes up to a day to harden completely. In assembling a joint, glue frequently seeps out from between the joining surfaces, and this should be wiped away as quickly as possible with a damp cloth before it has a chance to go hard.

In deciding which sort of glue to use, it is purely a question of personal preference, and this book does not attempt to make a recommendation. However, if you are undecided, you may wish to consider making a couple of trial joints and using a different wood glue for each in order to determine which, in your opinion, is more suitable for the project you have in mind.

CHAPTER 3

Ornamental Fencing

The idea of ornamental fencing is to give a simple and attractive decorative boundary to a lawn or flowerbed, but it also has a more practical purpose. If made in several sections, it can provide you with a temporary or permanent means of fencing off part of the garden so that you could prevent a small child, for example, from wandering close to an unprotected garden pool, or indeed, you could create a safe playing area on the lawn for a toddler. Depending on its use, you are free to build it to whatever height and length you wish.

Several lengths could be locked together at their ends with screw-eyes, nuts and bolts to form a square or rectangular enclosure. However, even if put to such a use, no small child should be left unsupervised, especially if it is used to fence off a pond or some other water feature, as these inevitably present a great danger to young children.

The fencing consists of no more than two horizontal crosspieces supporting a series of uprights that are each given rounded top ends. The crosspieces are

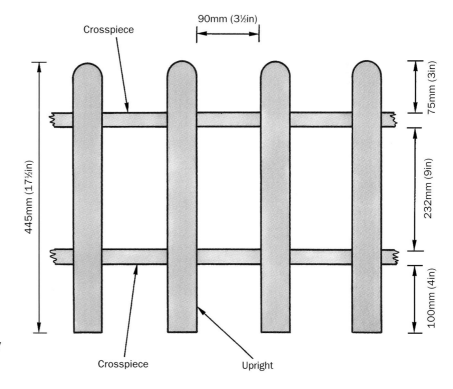

Front elevation.

OPPOSITE: *The finished ornamental fencing.*

Ornamental Fencing Cutting List	
Upright:	Twenty-four of 445 × 45 × 19mm (17½ × 1¾ × ¾in)
Crosspiece:	Two of 1,550 × 19 × 19mm (61 × ¾ × ¾in)

cut from 19 × 19mm (¾ × ¾in) softwood, and the uprights are made from 45 × 19mm (1¾ × ¾in) material.

In order to produce a rigid structure, the components are assembled by cutting housing notches in the uprights into which the crosspieces fit, each joint being secured with a dowel.

PLANNING AND CUTTING

Commence by determining how long the fence should be, and how many sections are required. The illustrated example has twelve uprights, spaced at regular intervals 90mm (3½in) apart. The uprights all measure 445mm (17½in) in overall length.

Using a tape measure, square and pencil, measure and mark each upright to length on 45 × 19mm (1¾ × ¾in) material, rounding off the top end with a pair of geometrical compasses set to a radius of 22mm (⅞in). Cut the twelve uprights to length with the jigsaw, working it carefully around the semi-circular curve with the blade positioned slightly on the waste side of the marked line, finishing off by rubbing down with medium-grade sandpaper. When all twelve

lengths have been cut, line them up in a row to check that they are all identical. On the rear face of each upright, mark in the two notch positions. Each notch is 19mm (¾in) wide, equal to the thickness of the crosspiece material; the upper notch is set down 75mm (3in) from the top end, and the lower notch is set up 100mm (4in) from the bottom end, which has been cut square. Set the marking gauge to a gap of 6mm (¼in), and scribe in the depth of each notch between the squared pencil lines.

Prepare the notches by sawing down along these lines, working the blade of the tenon saw on the waste side of each line, and cutting down as far as the scribed depth line. Chop away the waste with a 19mm (¾in)

Cutting a notch with the tenon saw.

Use a pair of compasses, or any convenient round object, to mark the end of each upright.

The waste is removed with the chisel.

Place the two crosspieces into the notches in the uprights to check that they fit before arranging them in their correct positions.

Marking a piece of dowelling to length.

chisel, working the blade firstly from one side and then the other to ensure that you do not inadvertently cut away too much material, and check to make certain that the crosspiece material fits snugly into the notch.

ASSEMBLY

When all the uprights have had two notches cut in each one, take two lengths of 19 × 19mm (¾ × ¾in) material for the crosspieces, allowing a little extra at each end. Place the material flat on the workbench and slot the uprights in position, arranging for a 90mm (3½in) gap between each piece. Make a pencil mark between each upright and its adjoining crosspiece, and in the case of the two outermost uprights, square right around each crosspiece so that its end will be flush with the outside edge of those uprights. Trim the two crosspieces to their correct length with the tenon saw.

Apply waterproof PVA wood glue to both of the notches in each upright, and join them in their pencilled positions along the length of the two crosspieces. Wipe away any surplus glue, and allow at least a day for the joints to set hard.

Finally, reinforce each of the housing joints with a single dowel, marking its position on the outer face of each upright, set centrally across the width of the wood, and midway across the thickness of each crosspiece, and drilling a 6mm- (¼in-) diameter hole to a depth of 25mm (1in).

Cut twenty-four dowels from 6mm- (¼in-) diameter material, each measuring 25mm (1in) in length, chamfer one end lightly with the pencil sharpener, and glue each dowel into its receiver hole, tapping it fully home.

FINISHING OFF

Rub down the completed fence thoroughly with medium- and fine-grade sandpaper, and paint it or apply a wood finish of the desired colour. The illustrated example is finished in white gloss paint.

Attach two screw-eyes at each end, adjacent to the crosspieces, off-setting them slightly so that their positioning on the one end is fractionally higher than at the other, thus creating an overlap, so that several fencing sections can be fastened together with nuts and bolts and remain perfectly level with each other.

If you merely wish to stand one fence section on its own, run a length of dowelling through each pair of screw-eyes with sufficient length to let you push 50–75mm (2–3in) into the ground. The tops of the dowelling may be decorated with small rounded knobs or finials.

CHAPTER 4

Flowerpot Holder

If your garden is very restricted in size, or you live in a flat and do not have access to a garden of any sort, you have no option but to look for alternative places in which to grow and display your plants. This simple flowerpot holder can either be freestanding, or it can have chains attached to it so that it hangs from a wall bracket.

The design is based on a square box with the four corner posts joined together by alternating side slats. The bottom of the box is made up of dowels arranged in a row, and this provides a platform upon which

to stand a medium-sized plant pot. If you wish to accommodate a large or small pot, the dimensions may be altered accordingly.

PLANNING AND CUTTING

Begin by selecting your pot, and measure the diameter to give the required distance between the inside faces of the opposing side slats. As the slats interlock on adjacent sides, you will see that one pair of sides has three slats, and the other pair four. Each

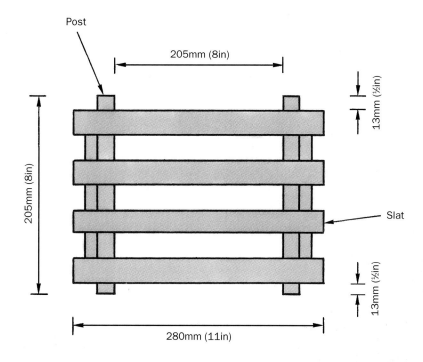

Side elevation.

OPPOSITE: *The finished flowerpot holder.*

Flowerpot Holder Cutting List

Post:	Four of 205 × 19 × 19mm (8 × ¾ × ¾in)
Slat:	Fourteen of 280 × 25 × 13mm (11 × 1 × ½in)
Dowel base:	Four of 216 × 16mm diameter (8½ × ⅝in diameter)

slat is joined at either end to a post with a single dowel joint.

The first step is to cut the four posts to length. The best material for the job is 19mm (¾in) ramin, which can be purchased from most DIY stockists, together with a quantity of matching 25 × 13mm (1 × ½in) hardwood for the slats. Each post measures 205mm (8in) long, and the two opposing sides that carry four slats have the top one set down 13mm (½in) from the top end of the post, and the bottom slat set up by 13mm (½in) from the bottom end. In between each of the slats is a gap of 25mm (1in), which gives just sufficient room to accommodate the three slats in the two adjoining sides; these in turn fit inside the four slats on the opposite side.

The fact that ramin is prepared to a width of exactly 25mm (1in) makes the task of marking out the posts much easier. Measure the slat positions and mark them in with a square and pencil, each post having lines drawn on two adjacent sides. On one of these faces, measure and mark in the four points that represent the centre of the four slat positions, and do the same on the adjoining face for the centre of the three alternating slats. Clamp the post in the vice and drill down into each marked position with a 6mm- (¼in-) diameter auger bit mounted in a handbrace, boring to a depth of approximately 13mm (½in).

Cut a total of fourteen slats to length, the amount

depending on the diameter of your chosen plant pot, to which you must add a further 50mm (2in). In this instance each slat measures 280mm (11in) long. Of the additional 50mm (2in), 25mm (1in) projects beyond each post. Mark a single dowel hole at each end of the fourteen slats, set in by 34mm (1⅜in) from either end. These hole positions must be placed exactly halfway across the width of the slats, otherwise they will not interlock properly during assembly.

Taking each side slat one at a time, clamp it on to a piece of clean scrap wood at the edge of the workbench and drill each of the dowel holes right through the piece with the 6mm- (¼in-) diameter auger bit. The purpose of the scrap wood is to serve as a solid backing, so that when the drill bit bores its way out through the opposite side of the slat, it does not split the wood but produces a clean hole. Drill all twenty-eight holes using this method, switching to a new length of scrap wood when necessary.

The next step is to prepare two of the slats to receive the four 16mm- (⅝in-) diameter dowels that make up the bottom of the basket upon which the pot rests. The positioning of the dowels is not absolutely critical, but they ought to be arranged so that they lie at regular intervals. Fit a 16mm (⅝in) centre bit into the handbrace and drill out all the holes. Do not bore right through the wood, but make a series of stopped holes. To do this, turn the drill until the pointed tip just begins to break the under surface – you will feel a tiny bulge developing. Do not drill any further, but clean out all the loose waste inside the hole with a 6mm (¼in) chisel to leave a neat stopped hole. Check the depth of the hole with the tape measure.

Cut four pieces of 16mm- (⅝in-) diameter dowelling to length, allowing for the extra required at each end to fit into the receiver holes.

Before assembly can begin, twenty-eight fixing

A slat with four dowel holes drilled at regular intervals.

pegs must be cut from a length of 6mm- (¼in-) diameter dowelling. Each peg needs to be 25mm (1in) long, and it is advisable to chamfer one end slightly by giving a few turns in a pencil sharpener so that it fits neatly into the joint.

ASSEMBLY

Start by assembling the two sides that each contain four rows of slats, making sure that you mount the two slats with the row of four dowel holes at the bottom, holes facing inwards. Apply some waterproof PVA glue to the dowel pegs and each of the holes in the posts, using a fine artist's paintbrush to work the glue thoroughly into the inside surfaces of the holes, and knock all the pegs into place with the mallet, driving them fully home. Check for overall squareness between the slats and the posts, because this type of assembly can easily become lopsided, with each peg acting as a pivot.

If the pegs have been cut slightly overlength, it is possible that the dowels will protrude a little, but the ends can be trimmed flush once the glue has dried completely, paring their ends with a chisel.

Fit the four 16mm- (⅝in-) diameter dowels into their holes and, holding the two assembled sides steady, glue and join together the remaining two sides with their three slats apiece, until the whole structure is rigid. You may find that it helps to have a second pair of hands available for this part of the assembly process. Any tendency for the sides to go out of square should now correct itself as you stand the completed basket on a flat surface, but whilst the glue is still wet you can make minor adjustments.

FINISHING OFF

If the basket is to remain freestanding, you may either coat it in clear varnish to retain the natural wood look, or paint it in a chosen colour. However, if the basket is to be suspended from a wall bracket, it will require four lengths of chain, each of which is attached at its upper end to a single ring. The length of the chain is up to you, but for guidance it is worth noting that it is usually sold by the metre. A one-metre piece, cut into four equal lengths, ought to be sufficient.

The chain is attached to the posts with four

Assembling one side.

Gluing the dowels in position.

medium-sized chrome-plated screw-eyes; if necessary, prise open the free end of the eye to enlarge the gap so that the chain link can slip inside. This method is better than cutting open one of the links, because the weight of the basket will probably pull the link open again.

Fit the screw-eyes to the inside face at the top of each post. These should be screwed horizontally into the posts rather than straight down into the end grain, because end grain is not strong enough to grip the thread, and the weight of a plant inside the basket will soon pull out all four screw-eyes until the basket collapses.

Slip the bottom link of each chain into a screw-eye, and join them all together at the top with a spring-loaded ring. The flower basket is now complete and ready either to be hung from an ornamental bracket or stood on a flat surface.

CHAPTER 5

Window-Box

The wooden window-box has become a comparatively rare sight nowadays, and one of the main reasons for this is that modern houses have shallow exterior window sills that do not provide enough room; and where a wide sill does exist, the window is often of the hinged casement variety that opens outwards. Thus the presence of a box would either hinder the opening of the window, or the action of opening the window would knock the box off the sill, depending on the size and weight of it.

Nevertheless, there are still a great many Victorian town houses that retain their original wide stone window-sills and sash windows, which slide up and down to open and close without interfering with the area immediately above the outside ledge. If you live in this type of property, particularly in the centre of a city or town where gardens are either restricted or do not exist, then you will certainly appreciate the advantage of the sill, which could be your only means of growing outdoor plants.

PLANNING

The window-box does not need to be a complicated piece of work – in fact, many early types were simply four lengths of timber nailed together, with a base made from a fifth plank with a few holes drilled in it to let water drain out. Our design maintains this simple outlook, but makes use of V-edged tongued-and-grooved boarding for the side and end panels; and the corners, rather than being knocked together haphazardly with nails, are jointed to upright posts. In fact,

OPPOSITE: The finished window-box.

much of the appearance is in common with the large Versailles box in the next chapter, although this elongated and somewhat squatter version has one or two notable differences.

The first contrast is in the way that the dimensions of the finished box are determined. For in the case of the Versailles box, as indeed with the flowerpot holder, the size is governed by the plant pot that you want to put inside it, whereas the length and width of the window-box are dependent on the shape and size of the window-sill. So you need to begin by measuring the width and depth of the sill, and since the majority of window-ledges slope downwards away from the window to allow rainwater to run off, you must also work out the gradient.

In the case of our sill, the distance between the side walls is 915mm (36in), and the depth measures 175mm (7in). The gradient is not always easy to determine, but probably the best method is to place a spirit level across the depth, adjusting it until it is horizontal, and then measuring the distance with a tape measure between the bottom of the level and the top of the sill at its outermost edge. A typical drop would be 13mm (½in), perhaps more.

To fit comfortably on the sill, the window-box here is built to a length of 760mm (30in), and the width at the base of the two sloped feet is 175mm (7in). The box itself is tapered when viewed from the end. Firstly, the feet taper inwards towards the base of the box, which measures 150mm (6in) wide, and then this changes direction and increases outwards until, at the top of the box, the width is 190mm. The top and bottom edges of the box are parallel – only the feet are sloped to match the gradient of the sill.

35

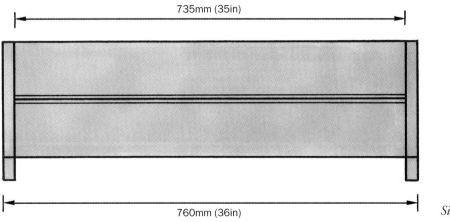

735mm (35in)

760mm (36in)

Side elevation.

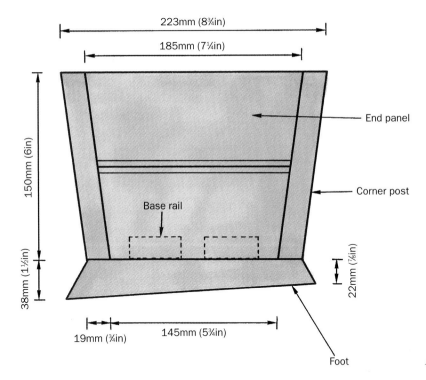

223mm (8¾in)

185mm (7¼in)

150mm (6in)

38mm (1½in)

End panel

Corner post

Base rail

22mm (⅞in)

19mm (¾in)

145mm (5¾in)

Foot

End elevation.

Window-box Cutting List

Corner post: Four of 150 × 19 × 19mm (6 × ¾ × ¾in)
Side panel: Four of 732 × 95 × 13mm (28²¹⁄₃₂ × 3¾ × ½in) T&G
End panel: Four of 200 × 95 × 13mm (7⅞ × 3¾ × ¾in) T&G
Base rail: Two of 710 × 45 × 19mm (28 × 1¾ × ¾in)
Foot: Two of 210 × 38 × 19mm (8¼ × 1½ × ¾in)

MEASURING AND CUTTING

The box comprises four corner posts, each with a housing joint groove cut along the full length of two adjacent faces to accommodate tongues cut at each end of the four panels. All four posts are cut from a single length of 19 × 19mm (¾ × ¾in) softwood which, for convenience, is grooved before being cut to length.

Setting the width and depth of the grooves is an important step, because you will note that there is only a small amount of wood separating the two. If you set them too wide or too deep, the corner of the post will be cut away completely as you prepare the second groove. On the other hand, if they are too narrow or shallow, the resulting joints will lack sufficient strength to hold the window-box together.

To prepare the grooves, you can use either an electric router, a hand-operated plough plane, or you can chop them out manually with a chisel and mallet. Whichever method you choose, the end result will be the same, but the router takes the least time and, in experienced hands, gives the best result.

Working with 19mm (¾in) square posts and 13mm (½in) thick, tongued-and-grooved boards, the ideal width for the housing grooves is 6mm (¼in), cut to a depth of slightly less than 6mm (¼in). The grooves, which should be marked with the mortise gauge, are not placed centrally across the width and thickness of the post, but shifted towards the outer edges, leaving just a small indentation between the side and end panels and the posts.

Set the pointers of the mortise gauge to a gap of 6mm (¼in), and adjust the fence to the position where there will be an indentation of merely a millimetre or so, and scribe the lines along the two faces of the post material. Prepare the grooves – either with the router, the plough plane or by hand with the chisel and mallet – along the entire length of the wood, then mark it into four lengths of 150mm (6in) each, and cut each post to size with the saw.

The total height of the side and end panels is 150mm (6in), to match the length of the posts, and this is made up from two tongued-and-grooved boards slotted together. The material will clearly need trimming along the top and bottom tongues and grooves before it conforms to the required size. Measure 75mm (3in) upwards from the joint line, scrib-

Preparing a groove with the electric router.

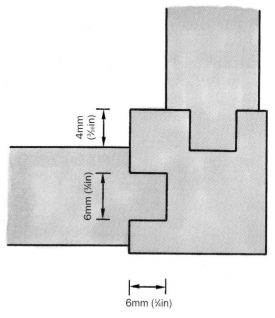

4mm (³⁄₁₆in)

6mm (¼in)

6mm (¼in)

Housing joint arrangement.

ing a line with the marking gauge, and plane down the top board, and 75mm (3in) down from the joint line for the bottom board, planing likewise, until the two boards, when slotted together, add up to a total width of 150mm (6in).

Now adjust the fence of the mortise gauge, with its pointers set to the gap of 6mm (¼in), so that it will scribe two parallel lines centrally along the end grain of the tongued-and-grooved boarding. Cut the boards into four lengths, each measuring 732mm for the side panels, and mark the lines at each end of all four boards to create the tongues that will fit into the post grooves. The tongues need to be cut to a depth of slightly less than 6mm (¼in), so measure this amount from each end, square off the shoulders with a pencil, and prepare the tongues by removing the waste with a tenon saw and chisel, in much the same way that you would cut a normal tenon. Make a trial fitting of each joint to ensure that the side panels fit into the posts, but do not attempt to glue them together yet.

As the two end panels are tapered, their preparation calls for a template, and this should be drawn carefully on to a piece of white card and cut out with a sharp craft knife. For each end panel, cut two lengths of boarding which, when slotted together along the tongued-and-grooved joint line, are larger than the template.

Now place the template on to the two joined boards so that its centre line matches up exactly with the joint line between them, and pencil around the card to leave a distinct outline on the wood. Cut the two boards to size, then mark and prepare the tongue at each end using the same method as for the side panels. Test the fitting of all the joints.

ASSEMBLY

The bottom of the box is made from two lengths of 45 × 19mm (1¾ × ¾in) timber, cut so that they fit between the two end panels, and fixed in place with

Using a card template to mark out the shape of an end panel.

A card template and the point of a nail are used to mark in the dowel positions at the bottom of the two end panels.

dowel joints, using two dowels per joint. Although the positions of the dowel holes may be determined by accurate measurement, it is a good idea to make a rectangular card template equal in size to the end grain of the base members, and mark in the centre of the two dowel holes. A bradawl or a nail can then be used to mark the hole positions on each end of both base members, and on the inside faces of the two end panels.

Cut the dowel holes with the 6mm- (¼in-) diameter auger bit, boring to a depth of 9mm (⅜in) in the end panels, and 16mm (⅝in) into the end grain of the base members. Cut eight dowels from 6mm- (¼in-) diameter material, each measuring 25mm (1in), chamfer the ends lightly in a pencil sharpener, and glue the dowels into the end panels.

Next, apply glue to the housing joints between the two end panels and their posts, and hold them together while the glue dries and hardens. Being tapered, this calls for wedges to be cut from scrap wood and placed at the extreme edges of the posts, before cramping up or applying a string tourniquet.

Once the ends are dry, remove the cramps and then apply more glue to the dowels so that the two base members can be fitted in position between the end panels. Knock the joints partly home with the mallet, but leave sufficient room to slide the side panels down into their grooves, gluing these thoroughly. When all the components are in place, tap all the joints fully together.

The feet are cut to suit the gradient of the window-sill, and these are tapered to match the width of the

ABOVE: Assembling the window-box.

A foot is attached to the window-box with dowel joints.

40

box at its base, spreading outwards towards the bottom sloped edge. Make sure they are identical to one another, otherwise the box will not sit properly on the sill but will wobble about – unless, of course, your chosen sill has an irregular surface and needs differently shaped feet to compensate.

Attach the feet to the bottom edge of the two end panels with dowel joints, once again using 6mm-(¼in-) diameter dowelling, setting the dowels at regular intervals, marking and drilling the holes in the customary way, preparing the dowels to a length of 25mm (1in), and gluing the joints together.

FINISHING OFF

Once the glue has dried completely, give the whole box two or three applications of clear or coloured wood finish, such as Sadolin, so that it will be well protected against the weather and the moisture from the plants.

On a point of safety, it is worth considering some means of anchoring the window-box to the sill if the gradient is particularly steep, or if your window is set high up above a place where people walk. Probably the most effective method is to fix two long metal hooks to the wall or the window-frame, and two screw-eyes to the outer face of the end panels, so that the box is restrained from any tendency to fall off the sill.

To accommodate your plants, you can either buy a plastic liner from a garden centre to fit along the entire length of the box, or simply stand a row of individual flowerpots inside. Whatever you decide to do, the finished box will bring a feel of summer to your room every time you look out of the window.

CHAPTER 6

Versailles Box

The best way of brightening up a corner of the conservatory or garden is to build a wooden tub, known as a Versailles box, and stock it with your favourite plants. The single main influence on the overall dimensions of the tub is the size of the plastic pot that is placed inside either to act as a receptacle for a number of smaller flowerpots, or which may be filled instead with earth and used to grow a small tree or shrub.

PLANNING

As the plastic pot forms the basis for the wooden tub, the first step is to visit your local garden centre and choose something that will fit nicely into a square box. It could be a conventional round pot, but an octagonal container would be just as appropriate, giving a greater volume as well as presenting a more interesting shape.

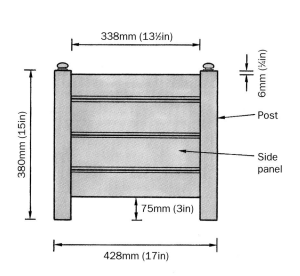

Side elevation.

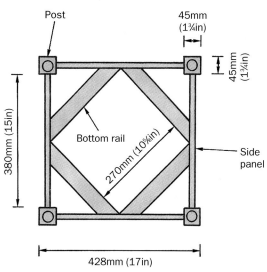

Plan.

OPPOSITE: *The finished Versailles box.*

Versailles Box Cutting List	
Post:	Four of 380 × 45 × 45mm (15 × 1¾ × 1¾in)
Side panel:	Sixteen of 356 × 95 × 13mm (14 × 3¾ × ½in) T&G
Bottom rail:	Four of 270 × 45 × 19mm (10⅝ × 1¾ × ¾in)

Measure the length and width of the pot, or its diameter, as the case may be, and the height from the base up to the top of the rim. These measurements dictate the internal size of the wooden box that we are now going to build, and it is wise to add a little extra so that the pot is housed comfortably inside the tub, rather than having to be jammed in very tightly.

MEASURING AND CUTTING

The construction of the Versailles box is simple, and consists of four corner posts joined to side panels made up from V-edged tongued-and-grooved boarding. Each panel is joined to a post at either end with housing joints, and braced at the bottom with two diagonal battens, making for a total of four battens altogether, which not only strengthen the structure but also serve as a floor support for the plastic or earthenware pot.

Once you have determined the dimensions of the tub according to the size of the pot, mark all four corner posts to length on a single piece of 45 × 45mm (1¾ × 1¾in) redwood. It is much easier to cut all the housing grooves for the four posts before dividing the wood into individual lengths.

The V-edged tongued-and-grooved boarding used for the side panels measures 13mm (½in) thick, so the width of the grooves to be cut in the posts can be set to 9mm (⅜in), leaving shoulders 2mm (³⁄₃₂in) deep to be cut later at the ends of each board.

Adjust the pointers of the mortise gauge to a gap of 9mm (⅜in), and set the position of the fence so that the pointers scribe the post centrally across both the width and the thickness. Along two adjacent faces of each post, measure in the lengths required for the housing grooves, and square off with a pencil line. In this case, for a post length of 380mm (14in), each groove is set down by 25mm (1in) from the top, and set up by 90mm (3½in) from the bottom, giving a groove length of 265mm (10½in). Score two parallel lines along the length of the grooves using the mortise gauge, making a total of eight grooves in all.

You can use various methods to remove the waste, as mentioned in the previous chapter. The simplest is to chop it out with a 9mm- (⅜in-) wide chisel and mallet; another is to run a combination or plough plane between the limits of the grooves (although since the grooves are stopped, this is not particularly easy, and the two ends of each groove will still need to be finished off with the chisel); and the quickest and neatest is to cut the grooves out with an electric router

Marking a groove along the length of the post material using the mortise gauge.

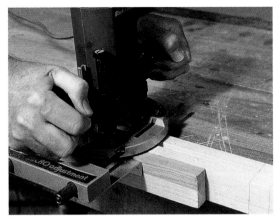

Cutting out the groove with the electric router.

A line is scribed along the length of one board with the marking gauge to show how much waste needs to be removed.

Use a straight-edge to mark the tongue positions at each end of the temporarily-assembled boards.

fitted with a 9mm (⅜in) straight cutter. But no matter how you choose to do it, prepare each groove to a depth of 9mm (⅜in), and when all eight housing grooves have been cut satisfactorily, saw the four posts to length.

Now divide up the 95 × 13mm (3¾ × ½in) V-edged, tongued-and-grooved boarding into sixteen pieces each measuring 356mm (14in) long. Some of these boards will probably have knots in them, as this is an inevitable feature of redwood. But the top and bottom boards for each panel need to be trimmed, and this gives you a chance to plane off the worst knots that lie close to the top and bottom edge, and will clearly have a bearing on how you arrange the boards in the first instance.

ASSEMBLY

Taking the joint between the two centre-most boards as forming a halfway point up the height of the panel, slot the top and bottom boards in place, making sure that they are fitting tightly together, and measure the total width of the panel, which is 305mm (12in), marking it in such a way that the two outermost boards require equal trimming to bring to the finished size. Scribe a line with the marking gauge on the two boards to be trimmed.

Clamp each of these boards in the vice, one at a time, and plane off the waste, effectively removing the

The tongue is marked on the end grain of each board with the mortise gauge.

tongue from the top board and the groove from the bottom board, planing down as far as the scribed line. As this entails quite a lot of planing, the task will be made much easier if you have an electric planer fitted with a collection bag to prevent all the shavings from flying everywhere.

When you have prepared all four panels, mark in the tongues at each end; these will fit into the grooves already cut in the posts. These tongues are 9mm (⅜in) thick, and can be marked along the end grain of all the boards with the mortise gauge; but you will need to alter the position of the fence so that the pointers mark the 13mm- (½in-) thick end grain centrally, leaving 2mm (³⁄₃₂in) of waste on either side. With the tape measure, square and pencil, mark in the shoulders of the tongues to a width of 9mm (⅜in) or slightly less.

Remove all of the waste using the tenon saw, in much the same way that you would cut a normal tenon, cleaning off any last traces of waste from the shoulders with the chisel. Check that each two-

45

Assemble each of the four panels to their legs to check that the joints fit perfectly.

BELOW: A batten is slotted into position on the underside of the assembled box.

Ready-made wooden door knobs add a touch of decoration to the tops of the posts.

shouldered tongue fits well into the grooves cut in the posts.

Saw off a portion of the tongue from the upper edge of the top board, and the lower edge of the bottom board, by 19mm (¾in), effectively giving these boards three shoulders, so that when all the boards are slotted together into four separate side panels, each one has an overall tongue which is slightly less than the length of the housing groove, which itself should be marginally less than the width of the side panel, so that the joint is concealed from view and makes for a good fit.

Temporarily assemble all four panels to the four posts, checking that the joints fit perfectly together and that the assembly stands on a flat surface without wobbling.

Now turn the tub upside down, and mark in the mid-point of each side panel along its bottom edge. Taking a length of 45 × 19mm (1¾ × ¾in) material, lay this diagonally between the mid-points of each pair of adjacent sides, working your way around the tub, pencilling in a series of 45-degree angles for the four bracing battens.

Cut these battens to size in a mitre box, allowing 6mm (¼in) extra at each end to slot into grooves that will be cut along the bottom inside face of the four panels. Use the same 9mm (⅜in) mortise gauge setting to scribe housing-groove lines along the four bottom boards between the limits shown by the pencil lines, and mark tongues along the 45-degree ends of each batten. Prepare the grooves with the chisel or the router, and cut the tongues with the tenon saw.

Re-assemble the components to check that the battens slot easily into place, forming a square pattern at the base of the tub, and when you are satisfied that all the joints fit well together, dismantle and prepare for final assembly. Apply waterproof PVA wood glue to the joints, commencing with the four side panels, joining these one at a time to the four posts. Fit the bracing battens, knocking all of the joints fully home with the mallet and a block of clean scrap wood, before cramping up the assembly until the glue has set hard. If there is any seepage of glue from the joints, wipe this away with a damp cloth whilst it is still runny.

FINISHING OFF

To finish off, fit a plain wooden doorknob to the top of each post as decoration. Each knob is fitted in place with dowelling, and only requires a 6mm (¼in) hole to be drilled with an auger bit into the centre of the knob's flat surface, usually pre-marked with a small pilot hole, and a corresponding hole bored into the centre of the end grain at the top of each post – this position can be quickly and accurately determined by pencilling in diagonal lines, the centre being the point where the lines intersect. Drill approximately 13mm (½in) into the knob, and 25mm (1in) into the post, and cut four 38mm (1½in) lengths of dowelling. Apply glue to the dowels and the holes, and fit each knob into position.

Finally, apply two or three coats of teak-coloured Sadolin finish, or any other colour if you prefer, which will give the wood excellent all-weather protection – and your Versailles box is ready to receive its pot plant and take its place in the garden or conservatory.

CHAPTER 7

Storage Box

The garden storage box is a useful item of outdoor furniture for keeping an assortment of small tools and implements out of sight but always within easy reach. It is made entirely out of V-edged, tongued-and-grooved boarding, with square-section timber posts projecting at the base to form short feet, and the lid is sloped at an angle so that rainwater can run off. The bottom of the box is a single piece of removable plywood laid on to four supporting battens. If you wish, this plywood panel may be covered with plastic sheeting to protect it from getting damp and dirty, as will inevitably happen over a period of time when the box is in use; alternatively you can just replace the plywood from time to time.

PLANNING

If the finished storage box is to be placed in a secluded garden which is itself secure, the lid may be arranged so that it simply lies in position without recourse to

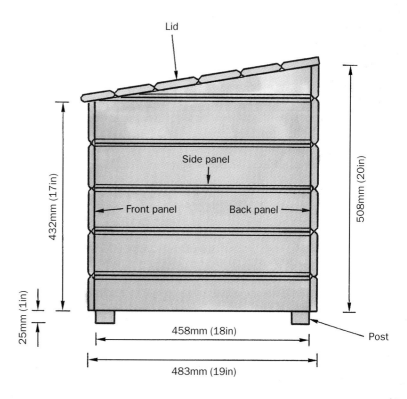

Side elevation.

OPPOSITE: *The finished storage box.*

Storage Box Cutting List

Post:	Four of 560 × 45 × 45mm (22 × 1¾ × 1¾in)
Front panel:	Five of 585 × 95 × 13mm (23 × 3¾ × ½in) T&G
Back panel:	Six of 585 × 95 × 13mm (23 × 3¾ × ½in) T&G
Side panel:	Six of 458 × 95 × 13mm (18 × 3¾ × ½in) T&G
Lid panel:	Six of 615 × 95 × 13mm (24 × 3¾ × ½in) T&G
Base panel:	One of 550 × 458 × 19mm (21⅝ × 18 × ¾in) plywood
Lid batten:	Two of 458 × 45 × 19mm (18 × 1¾ × ¾in)
Long base batten:	Two of 458 × 19 × 19mm (18 × ¾ × ¾in)
Short base batten:	Two of 368 × 19 × 19mm (14½ × ¾ × ¾in)

either hinges or a lock, keeping your gardening gloves, trowel, weeder, ball of string and other odds and ends in the dry and always ready to hand when needed. If, however, you require a more secure home for them, the lid may be fastened in position and kept padlocked – although the box itself will have to be fixed to a wall with screws in order to prevent it from being carried off.

Indeed, the use to which the storage box is put will determine how large it should be, for you can alter its main dimensions to make it bigger or smaller than the illustrated example. If you were to double its size, it could be used to house some of the bulkier garden tools, such as a fork or a spade. On the other hand, if you were to contemplate making it much bigger again, you might as well build a garden shed and be done with it.

The overall dimensions of the box are 585mm (23in) wide by 495mm (19½in) deep, and its height is 508mm (20in) at the back and 432mm (17in) at the front. Each of the four feet project 25mm (1in) below the bottom edge of the box. However, the height dimensions are derived from the fact that each of the V-edged tongued-and-grooved boards used in its construction measure 95 × 13mm (3¾ × ½in). By the time the tongues and grooves and V-edged chamfers are worked along their edges, the boards that you pur-

chase may be slightly different, and therefore when you slot several boards together to form a panel, the width that you obtain may be different to some degree. Your own dimensions should therefore take into account the size of timber that you purchase, bearing in mind that you must also allow for planing off the tongue, and the groove from each edge of the assembled panel, whether it is to be a back, front or side panel, or indeed the lid.

MEASURING AND CUTTING

The construction of the box does not entail anything other than simple butt joints, if you discount the tongues and grooves already cut in the boards, and the method consists of making the two side panels first, attaching these to the leg posts, preparing the sloped top edges, and then joining them to the front and back panels.

Side Panels

Begin with the side panels. Taking them one at a time, measure and mark six boards each to a length of 458mm (18in), squaring them accurately at each end, and cut them to size with the tenon saw or jigsaw. Slot them together in such a way that any knots are well distributed, and that the better of the two surfaces of each board faces outwards. Each of these loosely assembled side panels is left with a single tongue and groove, and the construction of the box should be arranged in such a way that the groove is retained on the lower edge of the panel, leaving the tongue to be removed. The upper edge is sloped, and this provides the opportunity to remove the tongue.

Place a straight-edged piece of wood in such a way that it runs from just beneath the tongue on the uppermost board, at its rear edge, to a position slightly below the tongue on the adjacent board, at its front edge, and make a pencil line to mark in the slope. Now detach the uppermost board, place it in the vice, and saw along the line to remove the waste portion containing the tongue. Plane the sloped edge to a smooth finish.

Leg Posts

Cut four leg posts to size from 45 × 45mm (1¾ × 1¾in) material, each measuring at least 560mm (22in) in

Six boards are cut and
joined together to form
a side panel.

A straight-edge is
used to mark in the
slope along the top
edge of a side panel.

Cut away the waste
with the handsaw.

Mark the sloped edge on to the legs in pencil.

length. This gives a little more than is needed, but the surplus will be removed later. Indeed, the two front legs are shorter than the two back legs, on account of the slope cut in the side panels, and you might think that it would be more economical to cut them shorter to begin with, and thereby save a little on timber; however, you may find it easier to assemble the side panels to the legs in a manner that is perfectly square and accurate if you keep them all initially to the same length.

It has already been stated that each leg projects 25mm (1in) below the side panels, so make sure that the bottom ends of all the legs are cut square, and mark a line 25mm (1in) from that end. Once again taking each side panel in turn, lay two legs flat on the workbench and place the side panel on top, with the outside surface facing uppermost, so that its two ends lie flush with the edges of the leg posts, the bottom grooved edge of the panel set up by the required 25mm (1in) from the end of each leg, and mark the position of the slope on the front and back legs.

ASSEMBLY

Prepare to fit the side panel to the leg posts with glue and nails. Start by dismantling all the boards that make up the side panel, then apply some wood glue to the abutting surfaces between the bottom board and the legs, lining it up carefully with the squared pencil line 25mm (1in) from the bottom of each leg,

then glue the joining surfaces of each successive board – in other words, the tongues and grooves, as well as the inside surfaces that butt against the legs, positioning them carefully to keep the overall structure perfectly square. Then drive in a series of 38mm (1½in) oval wire nails, two to each individual board; for maximum strength, the nails should be hammered in dovetail-fashion, as this will ensure that they hold more firmly. The glue merely reinforces the joint.

Once the two side panels have been attached to their legs, line them up side by side with the legs in contact with one another, and standing on the flat top of the workbench, to check that they are identical. Keeping them in this position, the next step is to mark the slope on each side panel. This is best accomplished by measuring and marking in the upper extent of the slope on the rear edges of the back legs, and the lower extent on the forward edges of the front legs in accordance with the fact that the highest part of the slope occurs immediately below the tongue in the uppermost board, and the lowest part is situated just below the joint line one board width down from the top. If you square across the legs simultaneously, this should ensure that both sides are treated equally. It is then a simple matter of separating the sides, drawing in each of the slopes with a pencil and long straight rule, and cutting away the waste with the handsaw or jigsaw. Work the saw blade fractionally on the waste side of the pencilled line so that the sloped edge can be planed smooth right down to the line.

Front and Back Panels

The front and back panels are made using the same method as that employed for the side panels, except that the back panel comprises six board widths, whereas the front panel has only five. Measure and mark all eleven boards to an overall length of 585mm (23in), taking care to ensure that each end is perfectly square, and cut them all to size. Once again, sort through them to select the best five boards for the front panel, since this is more prominent than the back panel, arranging them in a sequence that is appealing to the eye.

Prepare to assemble the front and back panel to the side panels, noting that their widths are slightly greater than required, due to the presence of the tongue along the top edge of both panels. However, it is easier to fit the front and back panels in place first and trim them to size once the assembly of the box is complete.

Accordingly, place the two side panel assemblies on the workbench, with the back legs lying flat on its surface, the two front legs uppermost, and lay the bottom board of the front panel in position in such a way that its bottom edge aligns with the bottom edges of the

Assemble each of the boards that make up the side panel, starting at the bottom and working upwards.

When the two side panels are complete, lay these upright on the workbench and start to assemble the front panel.

side panels, and its end grains lie flush with their outer surfaces. Fix it in place with wood glue and nails, driving these through the wood in the same dovetail pattern, and continue assembling the other boards to make up the complete front panel.

Turn the box over and prepare to fit the back panel in the same way. But before you attempt to make the fitting permanent, apply wood glue to the joining surfaces and tack it lightly with one nail at each end, so that there is still some freedom of movement. Now stand the box upright on the workbench to check that all four legs rest on its surface. If one or more legs are not quite in contact, it is still possible to adjust the alignment of the back panel until they are all level, at which point you can hammer in the rest of the nails, thus completing the assembly of the box. The excess width of the front and back panels, meaning the tongues, can now be trimmed back with the plane so that the upper edges form a continuation of the slope cut in the side panels.

Cut four strips of 19×19mm ($\frac{3}{4} \times \frac{3}{4}$in) wood to fit between the legs on the inside of the box at the bottom of the four panels to act as battens upon which the base panel will rest. Fit these with wood glue and nails, driving in the nails from the outside surface of the four panels. Each batten should be clamped in place as the nails are driven in.

Measure the internal dimensions of the box – its width being the distance between the two side panels, and its depth the distance between the front and back panels – and cut a piece of 19mm ($\frac{3}{4}$in) thick plywood to this size. Then mark in 45×45mm ($1\frac{3}{4} \times 1\frac{3}{4}$in) notches, one in each corner, to fit around the leg posts, and cut these away with the jigsaw. Place the panel in position on its support battens.

Box Lid

The lid of the box is a fifth panel made of V-edged tongued-and-grooved boarding, consisting of six separate pieces each measuring 615mm (24in) in length. Join these together with wood glue to form a single panel, and when this is complete, plane down the groove to leave a flat edge that will be at the back of the box, and carefully plane off the tongue, leaving the V-edged bevels, to become the front edge. If this is laid in place on top of the box, with the rear edge lying flush with the back panel, there should be an overhang of approximately 13mm ($\frac{1}{2}$in) at the front and on both sides.

The inside of the lid is braced with two lengths of 45×19mm ($1\frac{3}{4} \times \frac{3}{4}$in) timber, and this serves two purposes: firstly, it gives the lid some degree of rigidity; and secondly, it provides a means of locating the lid in a precise position, which is essential if it is merely placed on top of the box instead of being hinged and fastened with suitable ironmongery.

Cut each of the braces to a length that will permit them to fit just between the front and rear leg posts, with a fractional gap at each end. To fit them in place, lay the box upside down on the workbench – firstly

Fitting the support battens for the base panel.

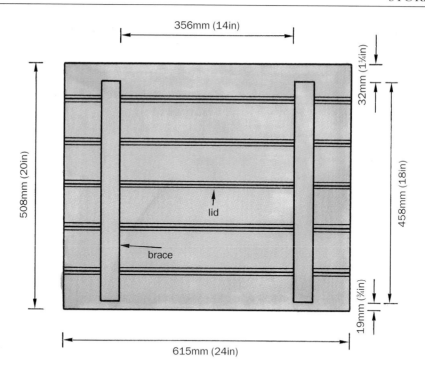

356mm (14in)

508mm (20in)

32mm (1¼in)

458mm (18in)

19mm (¾in)

lid

brace

615mm (24in)

Inside of lid.

removing the base, of course – and place the box in exactly the right position on top of the lid. Apply wood glue to the abutting surface on each of the bracing members, and place these on to the inside of the lid where they fit between the posts, and rest up against the inside faces of the two side panels. Lay a heavy object, such as a brick, on top of each piece until the glue has dried completely, and then drive a series of 38mm (1½in) oval wire nails through the top of the lid into each bracing member along its entire length.

If you wish to attach the lid permanently to the storage box, you have a choice of hinges: plain butt hinges are the simplest, but long strap hinges offer a stronger method of attachment, and the front of the lid may be kept fastened with a staple and hasp, secured with a small padlock.

FINISHING OFF

Whichever you choose, give the finished storage box the usual thorough application of wood stain and preservative.

Place the two braces in their correct positions on the underside of the lid panel before marking and fitting them.

CHAPTER 8

Child's Table and Chair Set

Throughout the summer, the garden often becomes a young child's main source of interest and adventure. For games, picnics, or when inviting a favourite doll or fluffy toy to a tea party, a miniature table and chair, or chairs, is the ideal equipment.

The designs for these two pieces of furniture, whilst based on full-sized tables and chairs, are deliberately kept as simple as possible. There is always a slight problem when scaling down from an accepted standard size, because the question arises as to how small the table and chair should be. The overall dimensions depend on the age and size of the child, and it is, of course, inevitable that the child will soon grow out of it.

The material used to make the table and the chair is ramin, a light-coloured and straight-grained

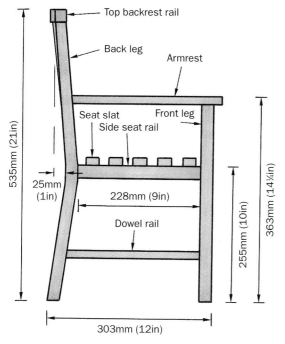

Side elevation.

Front elevation.

OPPOSITE: *The finished table and chair.*

Child's Table and Chair Set Cutting List

The Chair	
Front leg:	Two of 350 × 25 × 25mm (13¾ × 1 × 1in)
Back leg:	Two of 510 × 50 × 25mm (20 × 2 × 1in)
Top backrest rail:	One of 303 × 50 × 25mm (12 × 2 × 1in)
Bottom backrest rail:	One of 253 × 25 × 13mm (10 × 1 × ½in)
Front and back seat rail:	Two of 253 × 25 × 13mm (10 × 1 × ½in)
Side seat rail:	Two of 228 × 25 × 13mm (9 × 1 × ½in)
Armrest:	Two of 280 × 70 × 13mm (11 × 2¾ × ½in)
Seat slat:	Five of 305 × 25 × 13mm (12 × 1 × ½in)
Backrest dowel:	Five of 235 × 16mm diameter (9¼ × ⅝in diameter)
Dowel rail:	Two of 265 × 16mm diameter (10 7/16 × ⅝in diameter)
The Table	
Leg:	Four of 290 × 25 × 25mm (11 7/16 × 1 × 1in)
Top rail:	Four of 330 × 45 × 22mm (13 × 1¾ × ⅞in)
Table top:	Five of 380 × 70 × 13mm (15 × 2¾ × ½in)
Dowel rail:	Four of 340 × 16mm diameter (13⅜ × ⅝in diameter)

hardwood that can be purchased in a range of standard sizes from DIY shops; it is often supplied in 2,440mm (8ft) lengths.

CHAIR

Measuring and Cutting

Legs Taking the chair first, the front legs are cut to length from 25 × 25mm (1 × 1in) material, and the back legs are marked out on a piece of 50 × 25mm (2 × 1in) material, noting that there is a rearward rake to the top and bottom of each leg from the point where the side seat rail is attached. In both cases, the rake extends for 25mm (1in), and the legs are shaped in such a way that they are marked to a width of 25mm (1in) from the level of the seat rail down to the ground, tapering up to a width of 19mm (¾in) at the top.

It is possible that you will find it easier to mark out the legs if you first make a card template, and this is especially relevant if you intend making more than one chair and want to ensure that all the back legs are exactly the same. Whether you choose firstly to make a template, or to mark directly on to the wood, draw the lines clearly in pencil on both sides of each leg so that the shape can be cut with great accuracy.

Once the rear legs have been cut to length, there are various ways of removing the sloped areas of waste. One method is using the coping saw or jigsaw. The wood should be clamped securely at the end of the workbench, where it will need to overhang, and the saw blade manipulated closely to the marked line, just on the waste side. The use of either tool will need considerable care to ensure that the blade does not stray off course, and when the sawing is complete, the small amount of remaining waste can be removed with the spokeshave, or simply sandpapered thoroughly.

The alternative method is to plane off all the unwanted wood down to the marked lines – but this only applies for the outer convex curves. For obvious reasons, it is impossible to manipulate a smoothing plane on an inside concave curve. In this instance, the bulk of the waste is taken off by sawing a series of cuts down to within 2mm (3/32in) of the pencil line, and chopping away the wood with the chisel and mallet, holding the piece securely in the vice as you do so. A wide-bladed chisel should be used, preferably a 19mm (¾in) or 25mm (1in). Finish the removal of the waste by trimming down to the line with the spokeshave, and sandpaper the edges smooth.

Seat Rails The front, back and side seat rails are all cut from 25 × 13mm (1 × ½in) ramin, their ends marked square and sawn to length with the tenon saw. They are each assembled to the legs with dowel joints,

The back leg is marked out with a template.

Shaping the back leg with the spokeshave.

employing two 6mm- (¼in-) diameter dowels per joint. The rail positions are firstly marked on two adjacent surfaces of each leg, taking care that they are all at exactly the same height from the ground. For this, the rear legs must have their rearward rakes taken into account.

Square in the positions of the joints, which are all 25mm (1in) long, equal to the width of the rails. Set the fence of the marking gauge so that the spur scribes a line halfway across the 25mm (1in) width and thickness of the front and rear legs; then adjust the fence so that a line can be inscribed along the end grain of the rails, midway across their thickness. Set the dowel

hole positions in by 6mm (¼in) from each end of the marked areas on the legs, and likewise on the end grain of the rails, so that they correspond.

Mark the positions with the point of a bradawl, and drill to a depth of 9mm (⅜in) in the legs, and 16mm (⅝in) into the ends of the rails, using a 6mm- (¼in-) diameter auger bit. If the holes are bored any deeper into the legs, each pair will meet up with the pair drilled in the adjacent surface. This would not matter greatly, but it would be better to avoid.

In addition to the side seat rails, the front and back legs are also joined near the bottom by a length of 16mm- (⅝in-) diameter dowelling, which serves to

59

Assembling a chair side.

strengthen each of the side assemblies, and thus cope with the inevitable tilting back of the chair when it is in use – a habit, incidentally, which should be discouraged.

Dowel Rails The two dowel rails are set 75mm (3in) up from the bottom end of the front and rear legs, and placed halfway across the thickness of the pieces. Again, allowing for the rake of the rear legs, drill out receiver holes for the dowelling to a depth of 9mm (⅜in) in all four legs. Measure and cut the two pieces of dowelling to length from 16mm (⅝in) diameter material.

Assembly
The next step is to assemble the sides of the chair. Measure eight 25mm (1in) lengths of 6mm- (¼in-) diameter dowelling, cut them to size and chamfer the ends of each dowel by giving a few twists in a pencil sharpener to make for an easier entry into the hole. On that point, a word of warning: owing to the fact that some drill bits are made to imperial dimensions, and dowelling is cut to metric diameters, or vice versa, there may be a slight difference between what amounts to 6mm and ¼in. If the dowel is fractionally bigger than the hole, this could place a strain on the rail – which is, after all, only 13mm (½in) thick – and split the wood.

Make a trial fitting with a piece of scrap 25 × 13mm (1 × ½in) ramin and a piece of 6mm- (¼in-)

diameter dowelling: if the dowel does not slip easily into its drilled hole, reduce its diameter a little by paring down around its circumference with a small chisel until it fits without requiring any great pressure. Do the same for all the dowels.

Assembling the Sides Now for the process of assembling the sides. Apply waterproof PVA wood glue by brush to the dowel pegs and their receiver holes for the side rails to the front and rear legs, and for the 16mm- (⅝in-) diameter dowel rails and their holes. Tap the two side assemblies together gently with the mallet. They should, of course, be identical when placed side by side, and a comparison may be made to ensure that they are equal. Do not lay them one on top of the other whilst the joints dry, for there is always the possibility that some of the glue might seep out from the joints in the uppermost assembly and run down on to the one below, with the unfortunate consequence of sticking the two sides together. In fact, any traces of glue seepage should be wiped away with a damp cloth promptly, before the glue sets.

Making the Backrest When the two side assemblies have dried completely, prepare to join them together with the front and back seat rails. But before proceeding with this stage, note that the backrest must also be made from a top and bottom backrest rail and five lengths of regularly spaced dowelling. The bottom backrest rail is merely a duplication of the front and back seat rails, being cut to the same length from 25 × 13mm (1 × ½in) ramin, only that instead of being mounted vertically with respect to its width, this rail is set just off the horizontal, the small angle being accounted for by the rake of the rear legs.

The top backrest rail is cut from more 50 × 25mm (2 × 1in) ramin, and this extends across the full width of the chair to cover the top end grain of both rear legs. It is given a gentle curve backwards to make for a more comfortable sitting posture. The shaping can either be determined by measurement, or a template drawn up and cut out, particularly if you are intending to make a set of chairs, to guarantee consistency. Once the top backrest rail has been marked, cut and trimmed to the desired shape, it is given a single 6mm- (¼in-) diameter dowel joint into the top of each rear leg.

The backrest rails, five in number, are all cut from 16mm- (⅝in-) diameter dowelling and set at regular intervals in receiver holes drilled in the underside of the top backrest rail and the top side of the bottom rail. Clearly, as the bottom rail is only 13mm (½in) thick, the holes can only be shallow, and should be bored to a depth of no more than 6mm (¼in). Those in the top backrest rail may be drilled deeper.

Cut the five dowels accurately to length and make a trial fitting to ensure that the two backrest rails align with their positions, the bottom rail having its dowel joint holes measured and cut 50mm (2in) above the back seat rail. Prepare the dowel pegs as previously, apply wood glue to the various joining surfaces, and assemble in the following order: start with the front and back seat rails, and the bottom backrest rail, tapping the joints fully home; then apply glue to the receiver holes for the five backrest dowels, and to the dowel joints that secure the top backrest rail to the top of the two rear legs.

Bring the whole backrest assembly together, placing the dowels in their holes, before knocking the top rail down into position.

Assembling the Armrests The armrests are shaped in such a way that they commence at a maximum width of 50mm (2in) at the front, and taper gradually inwards to a width of 25mm (1in) at the point where they meet the rear legs. Measure and mark them on a piece of 70 × 13mm (2¾ × ½in) ramin, and cut them to size with the saw, planing the sloped edges smooth, and bevelling the rear end grain to match the rake of the rear legs.

Mark two 6mm- (¼in-) diameter dowel joints on the rear end grain and the rear leg, and a single dowel joining the top of the front leg to the underside of the armrest, arranging the position of the armrest in such a manner that its inner edge lies flush with the inner edge of the leg. Glue the joints together and fit the two armrests.

Cut the five seat slats from 25 × 13mm (1 × ½in) ramin, and arrange them at regular intervals between the two side seat rails, gluing them in position.

Finishing Off
Sandpaper all the corners to round them off, paying particular attention to the top of the backrest and the front end of the armrests, where sharp corners could cause injury to a young child.

Choose a suitable varnish for the surfaces of the chair. There is a wide variety of finishes on the market, some containing stains that will darken the ramin to any desired shade. As the chair is intended for outdoor use and could easily be left out in the garden, a water-resisting finish would be the most appropriate; and being a child's chair, perhaps it would be best to select the lightest possible colour, or simply use a clear satin varnish.

Assembling the backrest.

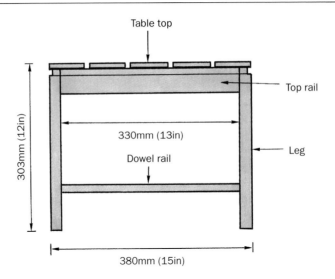

Side elevation.

TABLE

The matching table resembles the chair in several respects, most notably in the general method of construction. In terms of size, its height is slightly greater than the distance from the ground up to the seat of the chair, the difference being no more than 38mm (1½in). The table top is square, and composed of slats mounted on a simple framework that bears a close likeness to the construction of the lower part of the chair.

Cutting and Marking Out
To build the table, begin by cutting the four legs to length from 25 × 25mm (1 × 1in) ramin, making sure

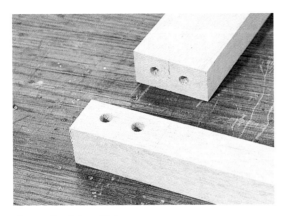

A completed dowel joint.

that the ends are perfectly square. Now cut the four identical top rails to length from 45 × 22mm (1¾ × ⅞in) material. The rails are dowel-jointed to the legs, their inner surfaces being arranged to lie flush so that, when viewed from the outside, the rails are set back by 3mm (⅛in) from the outer edges of the legs. The dowel joints are marked in the usual way with the marking gauge, tape measure and pencil, using two 6mm- (¼in-) diameter dowels per joint as before, but this time set in by 16mm (⅝in) from the edges of the rails. With the top edge of each rail aligning with the top end of each leg, mark the corresponding dowel positions on two adjacent surfaces of all four legs, and bore out the holes with the 6mm- (¼in-) diameter auger bit.

Strengthen the bottom of the legs with dowel rails cut from 16mm- (⅝in-) diameter ramin dowelling, drilling their receiver holes 75mm (3in) up from ground level, as with the chair, but on this occasion run a dowel between each of the legs, making for a total of four rails instead of two.

Before assembling the top rails, rebate the upper outside edge along each rail, taking in the top of the leg as well. The amount to be rebated is 6mm (¼in) wide by 6mm (¼in) deep for the legs, but since the rails are set back by 3mm (⅛in) from the outer surfaces of the legs, their rebates will be 6mm (¼in) wide by 3mm (⅛in) deep.

Mark in the rebates with squared pencil lines on the legs and inscribed marking-gauge lines along the

Cutting a rebate in the rail.

Placing the table-top slats in position.

rails; remove the waste with the tenon saw and plough plane respectively. In the absence of a plough plane, the rail rebates may be sawn out and cleaned up with the chisel, or prepared with an electric router – though with the router, it would probably be better to cut the rebate along a single length of material, before the rails are cut to their individual lengths. However, as the material is of small dimensions, it will tend to flex as the router is run along its length unless it is properly supported, and you may find it easier to mount each cut length of rail in a specially made wooden jig, using the dowel holes bored in the ends to support it, and clamp the jig in the workbench vice. There are various options available to you.

Assembly

Cut sixteen 6mm- (¼in-) diameter dowel pegs to a length of 25mm (1in) each, chamfering the ends and trimming where necessary, and then apply a small quantity of wood glue to each of the joints in turn and assemble the table framework. Cramp up the assembly until the glue has set hard.

Once the cramps have been removed, cut the slats for the table top from the 75 × 13mm (3 × ½in) ramin, and arrange them regularly on top of the framework. Mark in their positions with faint pencil lines, and assemble them with wood glue. There is no need to screw them in place or use dowels, as the glue should be strong enough to make for a lasting butt joint at each point where the underside of a slat touches the framework.

Finishing Off

As with the chair, rub down all edges and corners with sandpaper, and apply a matching wood finish.

CHAPTER 9

Small Folding Rectangular Table

This small outdoor table is useful for the garden, and as the folding legs tuck neatly into the frame, it is also well suited for picnics. The example shown here is made from iroko, a very strong and durable hardwood; although it works quite easily by hand, it has a dulling effect on sharp-edged tools. Other hardwoods worth considering would be sapele and possibly oak.

Mortise and tenon joints are used for the table-top assembly, and the legs and crossbars are put together with halved joints. None of these is especially complicated; rather, they rely on accurate measurement. The table-top assembly, although it may look complicated, is merely two side members jointed to two crosspieces to form the rectangular frame, with six slats, regularly spaced apart, running between the crosspieces to form the table. The leg assemblies are hinged to the side members with simple bolts and wing-nuts.

MEASURING AND CUTTING

The Side Members
Starting with the two side members, firstly measure in the position of the mortises, one at each end. These should be set in by 25mm (1in) from both ends of each side member, leaving an overhang; indeed, if you cut the two sides even longer, this will permit a greater

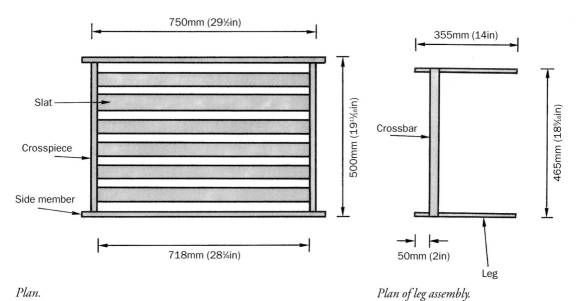

Plan.

Plan of leg assembly.

OPPOSITE: *The finished folding table.*

Small Folding Rectangular Table Cutting List

Side member:	Two of 800 × 32 × 16mm (31½ × 1¼ × ⅝in)
Crosspiece:	Two of 492 × 32 × 16mm (19⅜ × 1¼ × ⅝in)
Slat:	Six of 734 × 48 × 16mm (28⅞ × 1⅞ × ⅝in)
Leg:	Four of 355 × 32 × 16mm (14 × 1¼ × ⅝in)
Crossbar:	Two of 465 × 25 × 13mm (18⁵⁄₁₆ × 1 × ½in)

margin of waste, and the excess can later be cut off when the table is finished. By creating a 25mm (1in) overhang, the joint with the crosspiece is strengthened.

As the mortises and tenons are to be concealed from view in the completed table, the joints may be described as four-shouldered and stopped, which means that each tenon is formed by having waste cut from both the sides and edges of the wood in which it is cut, and the receiving mortise does not pass right through the thickness of the side members.

Chop out the mortises in the side members to a depth of 13mm (½in) using the 9mm (⅜in) chisel, and

Making a test fit of the mortise and tenon joint.

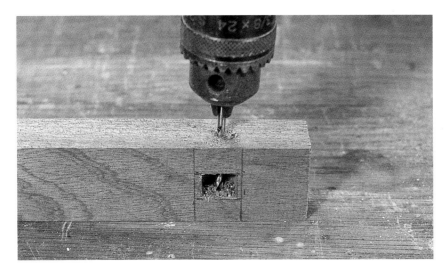

The completed hole for draw-boring the joint.

The completed bare-faced tenon cut in a table-top slat.

then measure and mark matching four-shouldered tenons at both ends of the two crosspieces, cutting away the waste with the tenon saw. Make a test fit of the joints to ensure that they fit perfectly together. During final assembly, each joint is strengthened by draw-boring, but as each mortise and tenon is comparatively small, rather than pegging the joint with dowels, small brass screws are used instead. Make the holes with a 2mm (³⁄₃₂in) twist drill, boring from the underside of the table top and countersinking for the head of the screw. However, do not assemble yet.

Fitting the Slats

Prepare to fit the six slats, measuring and marking a series of six mortises on each of the inside edges of the two crosspieces. You can determine your own intervals if you like, but you must remember to leave room for the leg assemblies to be hinged between the side members and the two outermost slats, with sufficient space to tighten the wing-nuts that hold the legs in position.

The length of each slat, minus its tenons, should be determined by fitting together the two side members and crosspieces and measuring the distance between the inside faces of the crosspieces. It should be the same along their entire length, but small inaccuracies may have occurred in the cutting of the four mortise and tenon joints, or the wood may be slightly curved, and if so, any minor difference can be incorporated into the measurement of the six slats.

Mark and cut bare-faced tenons at both ends of each slat: this means that the tenons are three-shouldered – there is one main shoulder and two secondary inset shoulders. Check that all the joints fit easily and snugly together.

The Legs

Before cutting the four legs to length, mark in and drill a 4mm (³⁄₁₆in) hinge hole 16mm (⅝in) from the top of each leg, centrally positioned. At the same time, drill corresponding holes through the side members, noting that the legs are best angled outwards for stability – and this needs to be taken into account in the positioning of each hole.

When all four legs have been drilled and sawn to length, the top edge that would otherwise bear against

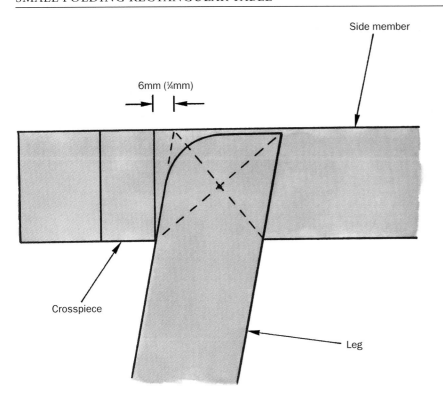

6mm (¼mm)

Side member

Crosspiece

Leg

Rounding off the leg to permit folding.

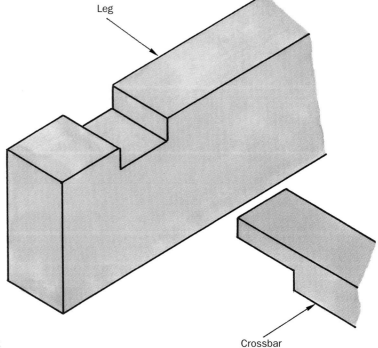

Leg

Crossbar

Halved joint for the leg and crossbar.

the crosspieces, must be rounded off by light planing, to provide sufficient curvature for the legs to fold up.

A crossbar is fitted 50mm (2in) from the bottom of each pair of legs using halved joints. Firstly, measure and mark the notch in all four legs, removing the waste with the tenon saw and chisel, and then cut a corresponding tongue at both ends of the two crossbars to fit each notch, so that the outer edge of the legs and the outer face of the crossbars are perfectly flush.

ASSEMBLY

Assemble the table top by applying waterproof PVA wood glue to the twelve mortise and tenon joints that attach the six slats to the two crosspieces, and then fit the two side members to the crosspieces, gluing the joints and draw-boring them by fitting a 2mm- (³⁄₃₂in-) diameter countersunk brass screw measuring 19mm (¾in) in length to each of the drilled holes. Note that brass screws are rather soft and can shear quite easily, especially if they are being screwed into a tough wood, so it is wise to cut the thread by driving in a mild steel woodscrew of the same size, then take this back out and fit the brass screw in its place.

Cut back the projecting ends of the side members to the required 25mm (1in) overhang.

Drill small fixing holes for the halved joints of the leg assemblies, and glue and screw them in place.

FINISHING OFF

When the glue has dried completely, rub down all the surfaces with medium- and fine-grade sandpaper, and treat all the surfaces with a wood dye. The illustrated example is stained dark oak. When this is dry, apply a suitable finish such as teak oil or polyurethane

The hinging arrangement.

varnish, depending on your preference. If you choose oil, give a thorough rub down with a good wax polish. Although this is an outdoor table, it is not the sort of item that you would leave in the garden when it is not in use – indeed, being a small piece of furniture and highly portable, it is likely to find a use elsewhere, such as the conservatory, and therefore deserves to be given a high quality finish that will bring out the grain and texture of the wood.

Complete the table by sliding the two leg assemblies into position inside the table-top framework, and hinge them with galvanized 38 × 4mm (1½ × ³⁄₁₆in) bolts, washers and wing-nuts.

The folding rectangular table is an easy and inexpensive project, and you will find that the table itself is as useful on a day trip or a camping holiday as it is in the garden and around the home.

CHAPTER 10

Square Table

The garden table that is square and has four fixed legs is most useful for a patio or, indeed, the lawn, as it is of a rigid construction and is ideally suited for eating outdoors, providing plenty of table-top space for plates and glasses as well as dishes of food. It is customary with garden tables to have a slatted top, since this allows for good drainage when the table gets wet either from the weather or accidental spillages of drink. For some reason, spilled drinks appear to be a certainty in the garden!

The design of this table is quite straightforward: it is made in two parts, consisting of the table top, a simple square frame with fourteen slats; and four legs joined by four rails to form a sub-assembly which is fastened to the table top with screws. The illustrated example is made of ordinary softwood, using standard timber sizes of 45 × 19mm (1¾ × ¾in) for the table-top components, 45 × 45mm (1¾ × 1¾in) for the legs, and 70 × 19mm (2¾ × ¾in) for the rails. These sizes are commonly referred to as two-by-one, two-by-two and three-by-one respectively in woodyard parlance, which relates to the measurements of the timber, in inches, from which they are planed to a finished size. You could, of course, opt to make the table in hardwood if you want something that is heavier and perhaps more durable.

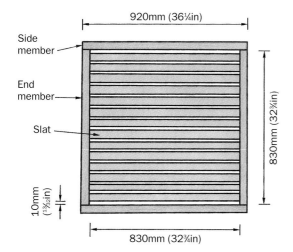

Plan.

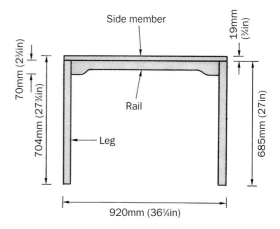

Side elevation.

OPPOSITE: *The finished square table.*

Square Table Cutting List

Leg:	Four of 685 × 45 × 45mm (27 × 1¾ × 1¾in)
Rail:	Four of 868 × 70 × 19mm (34³⁄₁₆ × 2¾ × ¾in)
Side member:	Two of 920 × 45 × 19mm (36¼ × 1¾ × ¾in)
End member:	Two of 868 × 45 × 19mm (34³⁄₁₆ × 1¾ × ¾in)
Slat:	Fourteen of 856 × 45 × 19mm (33¹⁹⁄₃₂ × 1¾ × ¾in)

MEASURING AND CUTTING

Begin by making the table frame. This should measure 920 × 920mm (36¼ × 36¼in) and is made up of two side members and two end members assembled with mortise and tenon joints. Into this frame fourteen slats are fitted, again using mortise and tenon joints, each spaced 10mm (¹³⁄₃₂in) apart.

The Two Side Members

Measure and mark the two side members to length, allowing a little extra at each end so that mortises may be cut without splitting the wood. A surplus of 50mm (2in) is more than adequate. Square pencil lines across to denote the required 920mm (36¼in) length of each side member, and mark in the mortises. The full length of each marked area will initially be equal to the 45mm (1¾in) width of the end members, but the mortise should be set in by 6mm (¼in) from the inside edge and 13mm (½in) from the outside edge.

Each mortise should be 6mm (¼in) in width, so set the two pointers of the mortise gauge to this amount and adjust the fence of the gauge to scribe the wood centrally across its thickness, and mark two parallel lines between each of the squared pencil lines. Chop out the waste with a 6mm (¼in) chisel, working from the centre of the mortise outwards, cutting to a depth of 19mm (¾in).

The End Members

When both mortises have been cut in each of the two side members, measure and mark the tenons in the end members. Bearing in mind that the completed table-top frame forms a perfect square measuring 920 × 920mm (36¼ × 36¼in), and that the two side members each measure the full 920mm (36¼in) amount, the end members, minus their tenons, measure 830mm (32¹⁹⁄₃₂in) long, to which 19mm (¾in) must be added at each end. Square a pencil line around the end of each piece to mark in the depth of each tenon, and scribe the pair of lines with the mortise gauge along the two edges and end grain.

Cut away the waste with the tenon saw, cleaning each of the two main shoulders with the chisel. Now mark in the secondary shoulders to match the setting in of the mortises – 6mm (¼in) on the inside edge, 13mm (½in) on the outside edge, and cut these away also.

Check the fitting of all four mortise and tenon joints so that the frame of the table top forms a square. Note that the small projections at each end of the two side members are still present, and should be left in place until after final assembly.

Making and Fitting the Slats

The next step is to mark in the position of the fourteen slats between the two end members. Each of the slats is fitted with mortise and tenon joints, so there will be twenty-eight joints to cut altogether. It has already been stated that the slats are all spaced 10mm (¹³⁄₃₂in) apart, with the same gap separating them from the side members of the frame, but you will need to measure carefully to determine the exact size of the gap rather than rely on the measurement quoted here, because you will need to take into account small variations in timber size.

Firstly, measure the distance between the inside edges of the two side members in your temporarily assembled frame. It should be 830mm (32¹⁹⁄₃₂in), which is the length of the end members minus their tenons. Now measure the width of each slat, which should be 45mm (1¾in), but there may be a small difference, either more or less, depending on how the wood was planed to its finished size. Multiply this amount by fourteen to give the total width of the slats, and subtract this from the distance between the side members. Divide this by fifteen to give the width of each gap.

Dismantle the frame, and, taking the two end members, measure carefully along each inside edge in the sequence gap-slat-gap and so on until the position of all fourteen slats has been marked in and squared across with pencil lines. By the time you arrive at the far end of the piece, you should be left with a gap of the required width. If there is an error, re-calculate and start again!

Retain the same setting on the mortise gauge to mark in each of the twenty-eight mortises, setting in each one by 6mm (¼in) at either end. Chop out the mortises to a depth of 13mm (½in) with the 6mm (¼in) chisel.

Once again, temporarily assemble the table-top frame so that you can measure the distance between the two end members in order to give you the required length of the fourteen slats, minus their tenons. If you have prepared the frame accurately, this distance should be the same along the entire length of the end members, but small inconsistencies can and do occur, and you may find that there is a difference of a millimetre or two between one end and the other.

In any event, it is a good idea to number all the slats, so that each one is cut for its own particular place in the order of one to fourteen; obviously if there is a slight difference in the required length of the slats as you progress along the length of the end members, this can be taken into account as you prepare each one. Mark and cut a tenon at the end of all fourteen slats to fit snugly into the mortises.

ASSEMBLING THE TABLE TOP

Make a final trial assembly of the table top to ensure that all the joints fit perfectly in place. When you are satisfied that this is so, prepare to glue all the joints together. Because so many joints are involved, you may require the help of an assistant. Start by applying waterproof PVA wood glue to each of the mortise and tenon joints between the fourteen slats and two end members. The process of assembly will be made easier if you lay all the slats side by side on the flat surface of the workbench, tapping the end members into place.

When this has been accomplished, apply more glue to the mortise and tenon joints between the side and end members, and fit both sides in position, knocking all the joints fully home with the mallet. Wipe away excess glue from the assembly and hold it firmly together with cramps or a string tourniquet for a day or so. When the glue has dried, remove the cramps or tourniquet and trim away the ends.

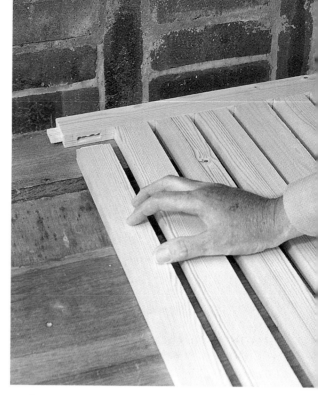

Making a trial assembly of the table top.

After the table top has been assembled with glue, cut away the projecting ends with the jigsaw.

Cutting and Fitting the Legs

Cut the four legs to length from 45 × 45mm (1¾ × 1¾in) wood, each leg measuring 685mm (27in). The rails that join the legs together are cut from 70 × 19mm (2¾ × ¾in) material, and each rail is shaped with a curve along its bottom edge in such a way that it retains its full 70mm (2¾in) width at both ends, but narrows to 45mm (1¾in) along most of its length. The legs and rails are assembled with mortise and tenon joints, the mortises being cut in the legs, with a tenon at each end of the rails.

The rails should measure 830mm (32⅝in) in length, minus their tenons. You may find it easier to make a card template for the shaping of the curve, so that each one is cut equally. Trim away the waste with the jigsaw, and smooth the curved surfaces with the spokeshave, finishing with sandpaper.

Mark in the positions of the mortises at the top end of each leg. In this instance, the mortises are 13mm (½in) wide, and are set in such a way that the rail is placed 6mm (¼in) from the outer edges of the legs. Set in each mortise by 6mm (¼in) from the lower end and 19mm (¾in) from the upper end, chopping out the waste to a depth of 19mm (¾in).

Measure and mark a corresponding tenon at each end of the four rails, scribing the two parallel lines with the mortise gauge, its fence adjusted to mark the lines centrally across the thickness of the wood, and cut away the waste with the tenon saw. Mark in the two secondary shoulders, trimming these also with the saw.

Make a test fitting of the rails to the legs, and place this sub-assembly on the underside of the assembled table top to check that it abuts in perfect alignment, with none of the legs projecting beyond the frame of the top. Once you are satisfied that the alignment is correct, dismantle the rails from the legs, apply wood glue to each of the mortises and tenons, and fit all the joints back together for the last time.

Final Assembly

When the leg sub-assembly has dried and hardened completely, prepare to join it to the table top. It is screwed in position with 63mm (2½in) mild steel Number 8 woodscrews, two per rail. Set the screw positions 150mm (6in) or so from each end of the rails, and drill a hole through the width of the wood, countersinking each one.

Place a screw in each of the eight holes, set the leg sub-assembly in place once more on the underside of

Mark the curve on the bottom edge of each rail with a card template.

Shape the bottom edge of the bottom rail with the spokeshave.

Fitting the rails to the legs.

The leg sub-assembly is screwed to the underside of the table top.

the table top, and drive the screws fully into their holes. If the table is made from softwood, each screw should cut its own hole as it passes into the table top, but if you have chosen a hardwood, you will have to mark each hole position and drill out a hole to a depth of 9mm (⅜in) in the underside of the side and end members of the table-top frame. It should not be necessary to strength the joints with glue – the screws on their own ought to be sufficient.

FINISHING OFF

The square garden table is now complete, and it only remains to choose and apply the usual wood finish suited to outdoor furniture. Since this table has fixed rather than collapsible legs, it is more likely to remain outdoors, and therefore it will require several applications of wood treatment, with further applications annually.

CHAPTER 11

Folding Round Table

A round folding wooden table is a particularly useful item of garden furniture, especially when it is complemented by a set of folding garden chairs of the sort shown in the following chapter. Its slatted top will allow rainwater to run off its surface if it is left out in the garden for a period of time, and if the weather is hot and sunny the centre slat has a hole drilled in it to receive a large sunshade umbrella. Finally, with its collapsible legs, it is easy to store away in the corner of the garage when not in use.

DESIGN AND MATERIALS

The design and construction is of the simplest kind, consisting of eleven slats for the table top, cut into a circle with regular gaps in between, and two pairs of legs that fold together in a scissors fashion. The wood for this table does not need to be of a high quality, and a cheap softwood such as white deal is quite adequate, any knots being concealed by the dark wood finish. However, if you wish to build a superior, heavier

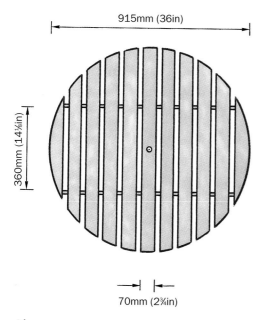

Plan.

OPPOSITE: *The finished folding round table.*

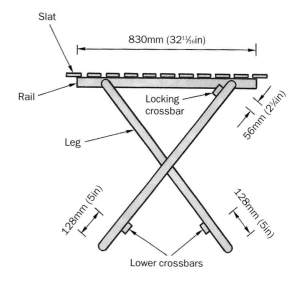

Side elevation.

Folding Round Table Cutting List

Long table-top slat:	Five of 915 × 70 × 19mm (36 × 2¾ × ¾in)
Medium table-top slat:	Four of 813 × 70 × 19mm (32 × 2¾ × ¾in)
Short table-top slat:	Two of 480 × 70 × 19mm (18⅞ × 2¾ × ¾in)
Rail:	Two of 830 × 45 × 19mm (32¹¹⁄₁₆ × 1¾ × ¾in)
Leg:	Four of 865 × 45 × 19mm (34 × 1¾ × ¾in)
Long crossbar:	Two of 482 × 45 × 19mm (19 × 1¾ × ¾in)
Short crossbar:	One of 450 × 45 × 19mm (17⅜ × 1¾ × ¾in)

version of the same design, you could opt for a hardwood such as afrormosia or even oak.

The overall dimensions are mainly a matter of choice, but the illustrated example should serve as a good guide, and keeps a nice balance between the diameter of the top and the arrangement of the legs. The *precise* diameter is dictated by the number of slats – eleven in this instance – the size of the gap between them, and the width of the boards. The marking out and cutting of the circular top is entirely dependent on these factors, so the exact diameter cannot be specified.

MEASURING AND CUTTING THE TABLE TOP

To begin with, cut the eleven slats to the required lengths from 70 × 19mm (2¾ × ¾in) material. Note that the figures quoted in the cutting list give three lengths: long, medium and short. Being a circular top, there is a diminution in length going from the centre slat to the two furthermost edges, but each length needs to be cut overlength so that there is something on which to mark out the circle. It is better to err on the side of being over-generous – though having said that, there is no point in wasting material unnecessarily. The rails, mounted beneath the table, should also be cut slightly longer than required, because they will automatically be trimmed when you cut out the circle.

The next important step is to arrange the rails correctly with respect to the top slats, and the only way to do this is by careful measurement. There are two details that you must get right: the distance between the slats, which is 13mm (½in); and the distance apart between the two rails, giving an inside width of 360mm (14⅛in). These measurements combine to make the table suitably rustic, and provide it with stability, which is the most important consideration bearing in mind that when it is in use, it may be called upon to hold hot meals and drinks.

The slats are located on the rails with housing joints, and fastened with glue and dowels – one dowel per joint – so that a rigid structure is created, which cannot be twisted out of square alignment when the table is in use. Without the housing joints, where each slat is set into two notches cut along the top edge of the two rails, the joint would only be held by the dowel, or alternatively a screw fixing, which could act as a pivot, causing the structure to shift into a lopsided attitude.

Making the Joints

To make the joints, proceed in the following way. Place the two rails side by side and hold them together with clamps; it has already been stated that they should be cut longer than required. With a pencil, tape measure and square, determine the halfway position of the rails along the length of their top edges and mark in the line across both rails simultaneously. This effectively marks the midway point across the width of the central slat, and as each slat is 70mm (2¾in) wide, you should now pencil in two more squared lines to mark the position of the slat, one line being placed 35mm (1⅜in) to one side of the centre marking, the other line the same amount the other way.

Having marked in the centre slat position, work outwards in both directions, leaving a gap of 13mm (½in) before squaring in the next slat position, carrying on thus until all eleven slat positions have been marked on the top edge of the two rails. The depth of each housing notch is 6mm (¼in), and it is a simple matter to set a marking gauge to this amount and to scribe a line on both rails – they can now be unclamped and treated individually – between each of the squared lines that mark the limits of each slat.

To cut out each notch, firstly clamp the rail hori-

Cutting the lines for the notches with the tenon saw.

Remove the waste with the chisel.

zontally in the vice and cut a series of shallow lines with the tenon saw along each marked-out area, making sure that you work the saw blade on the waste side of each squared pencil line. Cut down as far as the scribed depth line, stopping just short of it. Six or seven saw-cuts per notch should be sufficient. Chop away the waste with a broad-bladed chisel and mallet, working the chisel from one side of the rail and then the other to prevent splitting the wood as the waste comes away. Carefully pare away the remains of the waste along the scribed line to make a perfectly even notch, and repeat the same process for all twenty-two notches.

Assembling the Table Top

Although each housing joint will be strengthened with a dowel, it is best to glue the slats to the rails to begin with, in order to set them in precisely the right position, and add the dowels afterwards when the glue has dried and set hard.

Place the two rails perfectly flat on the workbench, in correct alignment to one another, set 360mm (14⅛in) apart, and arrange the slats in position without yet using any glue, simply to obtain the true position of each one. Remember that the slats have all been cut overlength, in three different categories, so that the longest ones occupy the central position,

Assembling the table-top slats in their notches.

followed by the medium-length slats and then the shortest lengths, each slat projecting by an equal amount beyond the two rails. This provides you with the basis of the assembly that, once fixed together, will be cut into a circle.

Ensuring that the two rails remain 360mm (14⅛in) apart along their entire length, remove the slats one by one, apply a small amount of waterproof PVA wood glue to each housing joint, and fit the slats in place, pushing them fully into their notches. Use the glue sparingly so that it does not squeeze out from the

Fit the dowels into their receiver holes to join the table-top slats to the two rails.

joints, because it will be hard to wipe away the excess without disturbing the structure. Indeed, the assembly cannot be clamped, but all of the joints need to be kept under firm pressure whilst the glue dries, so place some heavy objects such as bricks or concrete blocks on to the assembled table, with a few sheets of newspaper in between so as not to mark the surface of the wood, and leave it for a day to dry. If any blobs of glue have formed outside the joints, these will have to be trimmed away afterwards with the chisel.

Remove the weights from the assembly and mark in the position of the dowels. These should be set halfway across the width of the slats, with the exception of the end slats, where the curvature will trim away most of the width, in which case the dowels should be set 13mm (½in) from the inside edge. Mark the dowel positions so that they are also set midway across the thickness of the rails – you will be able to judge this quite easily by eye.

Drill each dowel hole with a 6mm- (¼in-) diameter auger bit mounted in the handbrace, boring to a depth of 50mm (2in). Cut twenty-two lengths of dowelling, each slightly longer than 50mm (2in), chamfer one end lightly in the pencil sharpener, apply glue to each of the holes and tap the dowels in place, allowing them to lie a millimetre or two proud of the surface. When the glue has dried completely, trim the ends of the dowels with the blade of a narrow chisel until they are all flush with the slats, and sandpaper the surface of each one thoroughly with medium and fine-grade paper.

CUTTING OUT THE TABLE TOP

The table top is now ready to be marked and cut into a perfect circle. Find the mid- point of the middle slat, both in respect of its length and its width, and make a small pilot hole with a panel pin at this point. The 'compass' used to draw the circle is a length of $25 \times 13mm$ ($1 \times \frac{1}{2}$in) hardwood batten with a 6mm- ($\frac{1}{4}$in-) diameter hole drilled at one end to receive a well-sharpened pencil, and a panel pin driven through the other end to serve as a pivot. The distance between the pencil and the panel pin is the diameter of the circle, which should equal the distance between the centre of the table and the outer edge of the two end slats.

However, the diameter must take into account the need to retain sufficient width of the outermost slats at the point where they join the rails, but equally, the full width of each outermost slat should be retained, if possible, at its widest point. If you have followed the

specified dimensions carefully, particularly the gap between the two rails, these conditions should be met. Place the home-made 'compass' in its pivot hole and draw the circle, taking care to manipulate it across each of the slats.

Fit a long wood-cutting blade in the electric jigsaw and trim away all of the waste, working the saw accurately on the waste side of the line. Apart from cutting through the thickness of each slat, which is only 19mm ($\frac{3}{4}$in), there will be four occasions when you arrive at the point where the end slats are joined to the rails, and the rails will be trimmed at the same time – hence the need for a long saw-blade. If the blade fails to pass through the combined thickness of the slat and width of the rail, the table may be turned upside down on the workbench and the sawing completed from the other side.

Finishing the Table Top
Sandpaper the curvature of the table-top edge until all the slats are perfectly smooth. If you wish to drill out an umbrella hole in the centre of the table, use the pivot hole for the 'compass': place the pointed tip of a 25mm- (1in-) diameter centre bit, or flat wood-boring bit, in this, and drill a hole through the wood. Do not drill right through in one go, but stop at the point when the tip of the bit just breaks the under-surface, then turn the table over and complete the drilling from the other side. This simple precaution prevents the wood from splitting.

Mark in the circular table-top pattern with the home-made 'compass'.

Cut around the curved pencil lines with the jigsaw to form the circular shape.

MEASURING AND CUTTING THE LEGS

The legs are made in a criss-cross pattern, with two pairs of legs hinged together at their centres, one pair being fixed to one end of the table rails whilst the other pair has a crossbar that fits into a slot cut at the other end of the rails.

The four legs are all the same length, cut from 45 × 19mm (1¾ × ¾in) material. Measure and mark each leg to size, noting that both ends are rounded into semi-circles, using either a pair of geometrical compasses or a suitable template drawn on to card and cut out with a craft knife. Cut all four legs with the jigsaw or coping saw, checking that they are all identical by laying them side by side before sandpapering the curves to a smooth finish.

The two pairs of legs are made up so that the inner pair is joined at one end only with a short crossbar, whilst the outer pair is joined at each end with a long

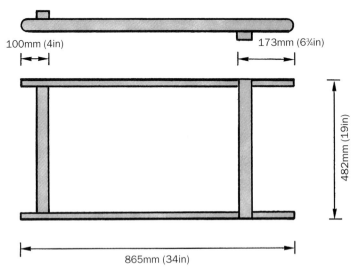

100mm (4in)

173mm (6¾in)

482mm (19in)

865mm (34in)

Outer leg arrangement.

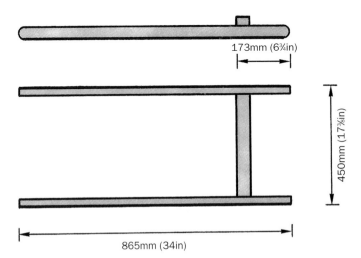

173mm (6¾in)

450mm (17¾in)

865mm (34in)

Inner leg arrangement.

A piece of waste wood is clamped beside the rail to allow the auger bit to bore cleanly through without splitting the underside.

crossbar. One of these crossbars is set close to the upper end of the two legs, which fits into the receiver slots that will be cut in the underside of the table rails.

Before measuring and fitting the crossbars, mark out the positions of the hinge-holes, comprising a 6mm- (¼in-) diameter hole drilled through the middle of each leg to join the two pairs together, and a hole at the top of the two legs that form the inner pair. Also drill a shallow 13mm- (½in-) diameter recess on the inside face of the middle holes and the outer-facing surface of the top holes in the inner pair of legs, so that when the hinging bolts are fitted, their heads or fixing nuts are set into the wood to stop them from catching against the adjacent legs when folded.

Assembling the Legs

The crossbars are fitted to the legs with dowel joints, using two dowels each for rigidity. Cut the crossbars to length, setting the two lower crossbars in by 128mm (5in) from the bottom curved ends of the legs, and the one upper locking crossbar, the one that fits into the slot in the rails, by 56mm (2¼in) from the top curved end. It is important to cut the dowel joints

accurately for all three crossbars, since there should be a gap of 2mm (3⁄32in) between the inner and outer pair of legs to facilitate an easy hinging action as the legs are folded and unfolded. Equally, the inner pair of legs needs to be hinged to the table rails with the same clearance.

Each dowel joint has a combined depth of 50mm (2in) through the thickness of the crossbar into the width of the leg. Cut twelve dowels to a length of 50mm (2in) each, and glue the joints together. Whilst the glue is drying, lay the table top upside down on the workbench and mark in the positions of the hinging holes: 120mm (4¾in) from one end of the rails, and the locking slots for the crossbar 175mm (6⅞in) from the other end. Note that the precise positioning of these holes may need to be checked when the legs are assembled into their folding configuration, held temporarily together with lengths of wooden dowelling, so that the correct geometry can be achieved, rather than relying solely on measurement.

The slots should have a card template prepared so that they may be marked accurately, and the waste cut out with the tenon saw and the chisel. A further

*Assembling a crossbar
to a leg with dowels.*

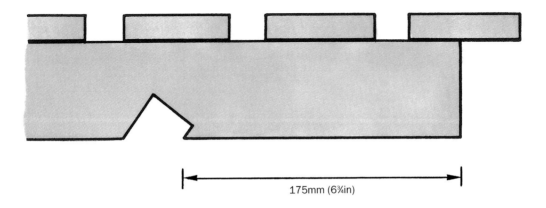

175mm (6¾in)

Side view of table, showing position of slot cut for locking crossbar.

refinement is to cut two shallow corresponding notches in the upper edge of the locking crossbar, so that there is no lateral movement when the legs are unfolded into their standing position. The lower edge of the locking crossbar also has a gentle curve cut along it corresponding to the curvature of the table top, so that when the legs are folded flat, there is sufficient clearance between the crossbar and the end slat of the table.

FINISHING OFF

When you are satisfied that the legs hinge properly, remove the dowels from the hinge holes and treat the table top and the two leg assemblies with a wood finish of your choice, giving two or three coats. Re-assemble the table with 6mm- (¼in-) diameter galvanized steel bolts for the hinges measuring 38mm (1½in) long, with plain washers to act as spacers, and nuts to fasten them together. By tapping down the threaded end of each bolt, you can prevent the nuts from loosening as the table is folded and unfolded.

The design may be modified slightly, if you prefer, to make a rectangular-topped table that consists of a row of slats, all of the same length, which have their ends rounded off for decoration, and which are mounted on the same undercarriage of rails and legs. In this instance, the table-top slats are cut from 70 × 19mm (2¾ × ¾in) softwood, and number fourteen in total, each set 13mm (½in) apart.

A variation on the design – the rectangular-topped table.

CHAPTER 12

Folding Garden Chair

This simple folding garden chair is designed to match the folding round table, and is made along the same principle of employing a criss-cross arrangement of legs to which the seat is hinged, one pair with a cross-bar that slots into the rails that run beneath the seat and support it. The difference lies in the fact that the second pair of legs extends upwards to form the backrest, and the front and back legs are hinged in such a way that the back legs extend further to the rear to provide as much stability as possible for the chair's occupant. Indeed the backrest, in forming a straight continuation of the front legs, has quite a pronounced backward slant, the back leg/front seat support angled at 45 degrees to the horizontal, and the front leg/backrest angled at 60 degrees to the horizontal. The seat consists of five slats dowel-jointed to the seat rails.

MEASURING AND CUTTING

The chair is made in three stages: firstly, the two sides are each constructed from two legs and a seat rail, which are mutually hinged; secondly, the two sides are joined together with three crossbars and two backrest rails; and thirdly, the five seat slats are fitted to the frame.

Start by cutting the four legs to length. The two back leg/front seat support pieces each have a 45-degree mitre cut at their bottom end so that the back leg rests flat on the ground, and the top end is rounded into a semi-circle; and the two front leg/backrest pieces each have a 60-degree angle cut at their bottom end and are similarly rounded at the top.

OPPOSITE: *The finished folding garden chair.*

The semi-circles should be drawn in with a pair of geometrical compasses set to a radius of 22mm (⅞in), or half the width of the material from which the legs are cut. Cut away the waste from the curves with the jigsaw or coping saw, and sandpaper to a smooth finish.

Likewise, measure and mark the two seat rails to length, inscribing a semi-circle at each end with the compasses before cutting with the jigsaw.

Mark a 45-degree mitre at the bottom of a back leg/front seat support piece using a geometrical set square.

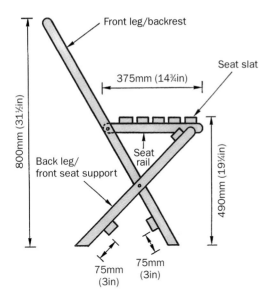

Side elevation.

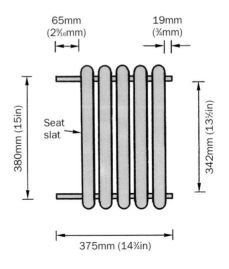

Plan of seat.

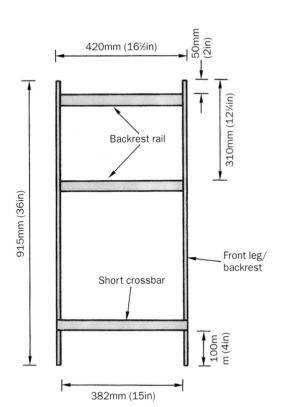

Plan of front leg/backrest.

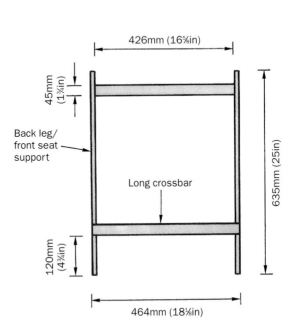

Plan of rear leg.

Folding Garden Chair Cutting List	
Front leg/backrest:	Two of 915 × 45 × 19mm (36 × 1¾ × ¾in)
Back leg/front seat support:	Two of 635 × 45 × 19mm (25 × 1¾ × ¾in)
Seat rail:	Two of 375 × 45 × 19mm (14¾ × 1¾ × ¾in)
Seat slat:	Five of 458 × 45 × 19mm (18 × 1¾ × ¾in)
Backrest rail:	Two of 394 × 45 × 19mm (15½ × 1¾ × ¾in)
Long crossbar:	Two of 464 × 45 × 19mm (18⅛ × 1¾ × ¾in)
Short crossbar:	One of 420 × 45 × 19mm (16½ × 1¾ × ¾in)

ASSEMBLY

Stage 1: Constructing the Sides

The hinging of the legs and seat rail is achieved by boring a 6mm- (¼in-) diameter hole through each piece in the marked positions and recessing each of the four holes drilled in the front leg/backrest with a shallow 13mm (½in) hole in the following positions: on the outside face of the wood where the piece is hinged to the seat rail, and on the inside face where it is hinged to the other leg. The purpose of the recess is to ensure that the hinge bolt does not jut out and prevent the legs from folding flat, as in the case of the folding round table (*qv*).

Make a trial fitting of a side assembly.

Once the hinge holes have been drilled, the two side assemblies can be temporarily put together with 6mm- (¼in-) diameter galvanized steel bolts measuring 38mm (1½in) long, washers to act as spacers, and securing nuts. Lay one side assembly on top of the other to check that they are identical, but in reverse sequence, to each other. When you are satisfied that they are the same, dismantle the hinges.

Stage 2: Joining the Two Sides

Taking the two front leg/backrest pieces, prepare to fit the two backrest rails. These are both secured in place with mortise and tenon joints, the mortises being cut in the inside faces of the backrest section, with corresponding tenons prepared at each end of the two rails.

The top backrest rail is set down 50mm (2in) from the rounded upper end of the backrest pieces, and the bottom backrest rail is set up 50mm (2in) from the hinge hole that joins the backrest to the seat rail. Each rail is set in by 6mm (¼in) from the rear edge of the backrest pieces. Square in the positions of the mortises using a tape measure, square and pencil, and scribe two parallel lines with the mortise gauge to a width of 13mm (½in). The mortises should be of the four-shouldered stopped variety, so that it is entirely concealed from view, the depth of each mortise being 13mm (½in).

Drill out most of the waste from all four mortises using a 9mm (⅜in) auger bit, finishing off with a 13mm (½in) chisel.

Measure and mark a corresponding tenon at the end of each backrest slat, cut away the waste with the tenon saw, clean all the shoulders with the chisel to remove all traces of stray wood, and make a trial fitting of the joints. The length of the backrest rails clearly determines the width of the seat. In this case, a length of 380mm (15in) for each rail, not counting the tenons, is considered most appropriate.

When you are satisfied that the mortises and tenons are fitting perfectly, apply some waterproof PVA wood glue to the joints and assemble the two

Tenons are cut at the ends of the two backrest slats to fit into mortises cut in the legs.

Fitting two crossbars to the back leg/front seat supports.

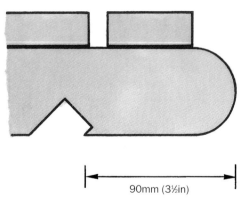

Side view of seat, showing position of slot cut for locking crossbar.

90mm (3½in)

An angled slot is cut into the bottom edge of a seat rail with the jigsaw.

front leg/backrest pieces to the two backrest rails, tapping the joints fully home with the mallet. Check that the assembly is perfectly square before cramping it up and placing to one side until the glue has dried thoroughly and set hard.

Next, fit the short crossbar to the back edge of the front leg/backrest assembly, setting it up 75mm (3in) from the ground. The crossbar should measure 418mm (16½in) in length, and is fixed in place with dowel joints, using two dowels per joint. Mark in the dowel hole positions on the crossbar, drilling them with the 6mm (¼in) auger bit, and then mark the

corresponding positions on the back of the legs, boring to a depth of 32mm (1¼in). Cut four 50mm (2in) lengths of 6mm- (¼in-) diameter dowelling, chamfer one end lightly, and apply glue to the abutting surfaces of wood as well as the dowels and dowel holes, tapping the dowels into place with the mallet.

Follow the same procedure for the two crossbars that are mounted on the back leg/front seat support pieces, noting that their overall length should be 460mm (18⅛in): this will leave a 2mm (³⁄₃₂in) gap between both pairs of legs when they are ready to be

Waste is removed from each end of the top crossbar to form a notch.

ABOVE: The first two parts of the chair frame are assembled.

The seat rails are added to the chair frame.

hinged together – a gap that will be taken up by washers acting as spacers. The upper crossbar, which will slot into the seat rails, is set down 45mm (1¾in) from the top of the legs, and the lower crossbar is set up by 75mm (3in) from the bottom. Fit both crossbars in place with dowel joints.

Taking both seat rails, mark in the slot position into which the top crossbar is to fit, using a card template to ensure accuracy, and cut away the waste with the tenon saw and chisel, or the jigsaw. Mark and cut a 6mm- (¼in-) deep notch at each end of the top crossbar to receive the slot in the seat rail, thus giving additional rigidity to the structure.

Stage 3: Fitting the Slats

Once again, temporarily assemble the chair frame with its hinge bolts to check that it fits together properly, and prepare to fit the seat slats. There are five in total, each measuring 458mm (18in) in length, cut

Seat slats are fastened to the seat rails with glue and dowels.

from 45 × 19mm (1¾ × ¾in) wood, and each one given the same rounded ends to match the legs and seat rails.

Place the seat slats in position on the two rails, the front slat mounted at the point where the rail curvature ends, the rest of the slats set at regular intervals with a gap of 13mm (½in) between each one. Glue the slats in place, and when the glue has set hard, reinforce each joint with dowels, fitting two dowels apiece. Drill out the dowel holes with the 6mm (¼in) auger bit to a depth of 50mm (2in), cut twenty lengths of dowel, and glue each one into its hole, tapping it in

with the mallet. Leave each dowel slightly proud of the surface, so that the excess can be trimmed away with the chisel and the entire seat surface rubbed down with medium- and then fine-grade sandpaper.

FINISHING OFF

Dismantle the hinges to split the seat into its three component parts, and treat each with three thorough applications of wood finish, matching that of the folding round table. When completely dry, re-fit the hinges, and the chair is ready for use.

CHAPTER 13

Bird House

Although most furniture for the garden is associated with the long fine days of summer, one item that comes into its own in the coldest part of the year is the bird table. This picturesque little wooden refuge is a place where you can provide food for the passing bird population. It has a flat base upon which bits of bread and a container of water may be put, it has a roof to provide shelter, and as it stands on top of a long vertical wooden pole, plastic dispensers with nuts and other foodstuff can be hung from its underside.

DESIGN AND MATERIALS

There is no limit to the possible variations in the shape and size of a bird house. This design is based upon a lych-gate, and is made up of four sections comprising the base, the two end frames and the roof structure. The fifth part of the assembly is the pole, but this is treated as a separate item and will be described later.

The two end frames are identical, each one being

OPPOSITE: The finished bird house.

The Bird House Cutting List	
The Bird House	
Post:	Two of 412 × 45 × 45mm (16¼ × 1¾ × 1¾in)
Crossbeam:	Two of 368 × 45 × 19mm (14½ × 1¾ × ¾in)
Strut:	Four of 216 × 50 × 19mm (8½ × 2 × ¾in)
Ridgeboard:	One of 430 × 70 × 19mm (17 × 2¾ × ¾in)
Rail:	Two of 430 × 70 × 19mm (17 × 2¾ × ¾in)
Rafter:	Eight of 268 × 19 × 19mm (10½ × ¾ × ¾in)
Roof covering:	Eight of 430 × 95 × 13mm (17 × 3¾ × ½in) T&G
Strengthening block:	Four of 63 × 63 × 19mm (2½ × 2½ × ¾in)
Floor panel:	Four of 430 × 95 × 13mm (17 × 3¾ × ½in) T&G
Long batten:	Two of 430 × 45 × 19mm (17 × 1¾ × ¾in)
Short batten:	Two of 343 × 45 × 19mm (13½ × 1¾ × ¾in)
Ledge:	Four of 343 × 19 × 19mm (13½ × ¾ × ¾in)
Ridge-tile:	One of 430 × 25 × 25mm (17 × 1 × 1in) L-shaped moulding
Supporting Pole	
Pole:	One of 2,100 × 45 × 45mm (82¾ × 1¾ × ¾in)
Long top crossmember:	One of 340 × 45 × 19mm (13⅜ × 1¾ × ¾in)
Short top crossmember:	One of 253 × 45 × 19mm (10 × 1¾ × ¾in)
Long top bracing:	Two of 202 × 45 × 19mm (8 × 1¾ × ¾in)
Short top bracing:	Two of 133 × 45 × 19mm (5¼ × 1¾ × ¾in)
Bottom crossmember:	Two of 610 × 45 × 19mm (24 × 1¾ × ¾in)
Bottom bracing:	Four of 305 × 45 × 19mm (12 × 1¾ × ¾in)

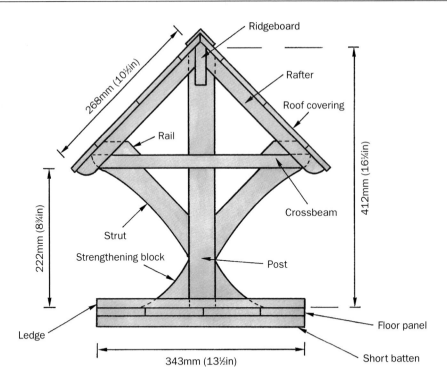

Ridgeboard

268mm (10½in)

Rafter

Roof covering

Rail

412mm (16¼in)

Crossbeam

222mm (8¾in)

Strut

Strengthening block

Post

Ledge

Floor panel

343mm (13½in)

Short batten

End elevation.

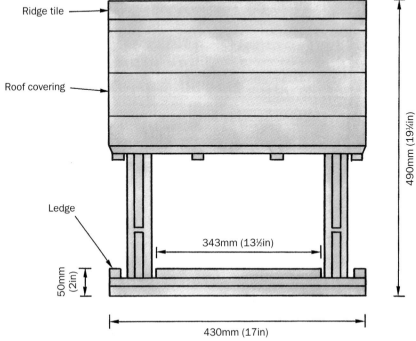

Ridge tile

Roof covering

490mm (19¼in)

Ledge

343mm (13½in)

50mm (2in)

430mm (17in)

Side elevation.

96

made from a vertical post supporting a single cross-beam and braced with a pair of diagonal struts. They are joined together by a ridgeboard and two rails, to which the rafters are attached. The roof covering is cut from lengths of V-edged tongued-and-grooved board-ing, which is fixed to the rafters. This assembly is then joined to the base and strengthened with triangular blocks. The rafters and the struts are arranged to form a square configuration, with a curved pattern worked on the lower edge of each strut for decorative effect. The timber can be either white or red softwood, both of these being cheap, and easy to obtain from your timber supplier.

MEASURING AND CUTTING

The End Frames

Taking each end frame in turn, measure and mark the main post to length, allowing for the two mitres that are cut at the top to form an apex, and the tenon cut at the bottom to fit into the mortise eventually cut in the base.

Place the post in a mitre box and prepare the two mitres with the tenon saw. Then set the two pointers of the mortise gauge to the 19mm (¾in) thickness of the ridgeboard, and adjust the position of the fence until the pointers mark the post centrally. Scribe two parallel lines on both the inside and outside face at the top of the post to a depth of 58mm, squaring off with a pencil line. Using the same mortise gauge setting, mark in the four-shouldered tenon at the bottom of the post to a depth of 13mm (½in), squaring likewise around the post.

Now measure and mark in the position of the halved joint for the crossbeam along the length of the post. This joint is constructed so that the crossbeam appears as a continuous piece when viewed from the outside. Cut the crossbeam to length, and mark in both parts of the joint, using the marking gauge to set the depth halfway across the width of both pieces.

Clamp the post securely in the vice, and start by cutting out the slot at the top of the post, sawing on the waste side of the two parallel scribed lines with the tenon saw, in much the same way as you would pre-pare a tenon, except that this is the inverse.

When you have cut down as far as the depth line, remove the piece from the vice and clamp it flat on top

Mitres are cut at the end of a post, using the tenon saw and a mitre box.

Scribing a pair of parallel lines at the top of the post with the mortise gauge.

of the workbench. Chop out the waste from the slot using a 19mm (¾in) chisel and mallet, working the chisel halfway through the depth of the wood before turning the post over and completing the cut from the opposite side. Finish with a clean vertical cut on the pencilled depth line, once again performing this from both sides to meet in the middle.

Check the fitting of the ridgeboard to ensure that the slot is cut to the specified width. If there is any ten-dency for the wood to bind, file away some of the waste from the cheeks of the slot until the two parts fit together smoothly and completely.

Now place the post back in the vice, this time with the bottom end uppermost, and cut out the four shoulders of the tenon.

Lastly, cut both parts of the halved joint between the post and the crossbeam, making a series of sawcuts along the length of each halved section before chopping away the waste with the chisel. Fit the two parts together to check for accuracy, filing off any surplus until a perfect fit is achieved.

Round off each end of the crossbeam, pencilling in a curve with a coin, or some such circular object, and remove the waste with the coping saw or jigsaw, sandpapering the curve to a smooth finish.

Next, cut the struts from a length of 50 × 19mm (2 × ⅜in) material. As the curve that should be drawn on their lower edge ought to be the same – indeed, there are four struts altogether – it is best to prepare a card template to ensure consistency. The curve may be drawn freehand, or with the aid of French curves or a similar drawing implement, and

The post is clamped securely in the vice and the slot cut with the tenon saw.

The waste is chopped out with the chisel, leaving the finished slot.

The curved ends of two crossbeams are marked simultaneously using a pencil and coin.

A card template of a strut is placed on the wood and marked out.

the template cut out carefully to exactly the correct size with a sharp craft knife.

Place the template on each strut, pencil along the curve, and remove the waste with the jigsaw, cutting on the waste side of the line. Now place the strut in the vice and complete the preparation of the curve with the spokeshave, finishing with sandpaper. Prepare the other three struts at the same time, so that they can be lined up in a row and compared for similarity.

Mark in a 45-degree angle at both ends of all the struts, using a geometrical set-square or a mitre square, removing the triangular waste portions with the jigsaw. Fit two of these struts in position against a temporarily assembled post and crossbeam. Mark in a single dowel hole at each end, drilling at right angles into the post and the crossbeam with a 9mm- (⅜in-) diameter auger bit, so that the hole passes right through the thickness of the crossbeam, and through the entire width of the post: if you are careful here, the two holes from each side should meet in the middle.

Drill corresponding holes into the struts to a depth of 9mm (⅜in).

Cut four 25mm (1in) lengths of 9mm- (⅜in-)

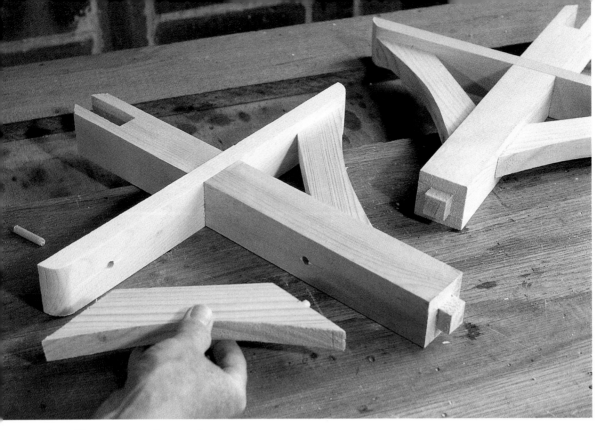

Assembling a post, crossbeam and struts.

diameter dowelling. Apply some waterproof PVA wood glue to the halved joint between the post and the crossbeam, then glue the dowels into their holes and fit the two struts in place. For this, the correct method is to begin with the dowel that joins the struts to the post, because once this is in position, the second dowel may be driven down through the top of the hole in the crossbeam. Wipe away excess glue and place to one side for a day while the joints dry thoroughly.

Use the same procedure to build the second end frame.

The Ridgeboard and Rails

Now take a length of 70 × 19mm (2¾ × ¾in) timber for the ridgeboard, and cut it to the required 430mm. Plane a triangular apex along the top edge so that when the board is fitted into its housing slots cut at the top of the posts, it forms a continuation of the 45-degree mitres prepared at each end.

Measure the two rails to the same 430mm (17in) length as the ridgeboard, and plane a 45-degree bevel along each edge.

ASSEMBLY

Fit the ridgeboard and the two rails to both end frames, thus joining the structure together. The ridgeboard and the rails should project 25mm (1in) beyond the outer face of each end frame to form the eaves. The ridgeboard is attached by drilling a 9mm (⅜in) diameter hole right through the joint with the post, gluing it into the slot and driving in a glued length of 9mm (⅜in) diameter dowelling.

The rails are fixed to the upper ends of the cross-beams with glue and a single dowel per joint. As these are being assembled, ensure that the two end frames remain vertical and parallel to one another.

Assembling the Roof Structure

The rafters come next. These are cut from 19 × 19mm (¾ × ¾in) timber, and each rafter is mitred at its upper end, where it butts against the side of the ridgeboard, and rounded off at the bottom end for decoration. Cut all eight rafters to length and mount these at regular intervals, the two end rafters lying flush with the end grain of the ridgeboard and the rails, notching the rails at 45 degrees to a depth of 19mm (¾in) and a width of 19mm (¾in) to receive each rafter. Apply wood glue to each mitre and notch, and secure all eight rafters with 25mm (1in) and 38mm (1½in) oval-headed wire nails.

The roof covering is made from V-edged tongued-and-grooved boarding. Treating each side of the roof separately, you will find that four widths of boarding, slotted together, give an excessive amount and therefore need to be trimmed. How you set about trimming the boarding depends on your own ideas of the final appearance, but the preferred method is to arrange for the join between the two middle boards to lie midway up the roof.

Mark and plane a 45-degree bevel along the upper edge of the top board, and a square edge for the bottom end of the lowest board where it should just overhang the rafters by 6mm (¼in) or so.

Apply wood glue to the upper surface of the rafters, and to the tongues and grooves of each individual board, and attach the roof covering, commencing with the top board, aligning the 45-degree bevel along

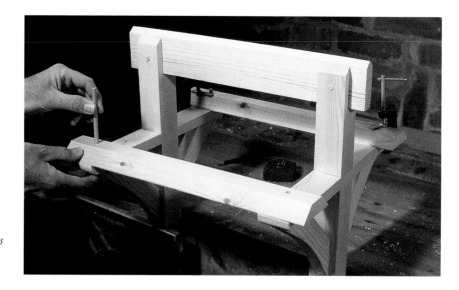

A dowel is fitted into its hole to join the rail, crossbeam and strut.

The rafters are fitted in position.

its upper edge with the apex of the ridgeboard. Fix the roofing board to the top of each post with two 38mm (1½in) nails, and then, working downwards, slot the next board into position and fix it to the rafters with 25mm (1in) nails. Do likewise for the third board, and finally slot in the fourth, nailing this to the rail with two more 38mm (1½in) nails.

Copy the same method for the roof covering on the opposite side, noting that the 45° bevel planed along the upper edge of the second top board should match exactly with the adjacent first top board to form a perfect right-angle.

When both roof coverings are securely attached, cut a 430mm long piece of L-shaped corner moulding, usually made from ramin, to form a continuous ridge-tile, and fit this to the top of the roof with glue and panel pins.

CONSTRUCTING THE BASE

The base is constructed from four more lengths of V-edged tongued-and-grooved boarding, slotted together to make a rectangle measuring 430mm (17in) long by 345mm (13½in) wide. Once again, the two extreme edges of the outermost boards will need

to be trimmed, and this gives an opportunity to remove the visible tongues and grooves, planing the edges square. Glue the tongues and grooves, and slot the boards together.

Cut the four lengths of batten that are attached to the underside, and mitre the ends to make perfect right-angled joints. Drill three countersunk screw holes along the length of each batten, equally spaced out, then glue and screw the battens in place, using 32mm (1¼in) No. 6 woodscrews.

Position the roof structure on to the base so that the tenons at the bottom of each end frame make contact with the boards. When the roof and base are correctly aligned, mark around the tenons with a pencil. Cut out the mortises within these lines, removing the bulk of the waste with a centre bit drill before chopping out the remainder with the 19mm (¾in) chisel. Place a block of scrap wood beneath the boards to prevent the underside from splitting, and test the joints for a good firm fit.

Cut four lengths of 19 × 19mm (¾ × ¾in) timber to make a ledge on the top surface of the base, with a gap left deliberately at each corner to allow for cleaning out occasionally. Fit the four pieces of ledging with glue and 38mm (1½in) nails.

Fitting the roof covering, which is fastened to the rafters with glue and nails.

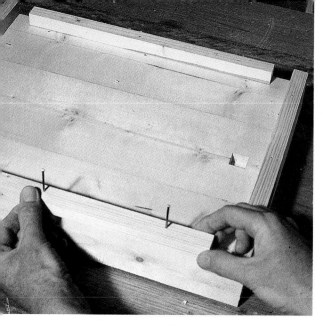

ABOVE: *Four pieces of ledging are glued and nailed to the top surface of the base. Note the gaps left at the corners for cleaning out.*

RIGHT: *The main assembly of the bird house is attached to the base with mortise and tenon joints.*

BELOW: *Shaped triangular joining blocks are fastened at the bottom of each post with glue and nails in order to strengthen the assembly.*

Cut four triangular-shaped right-angled blocks from some 70 × 19mm (2¾ × ¾in) material, working a curved surface on the outward-facing edge. Glue the two mortise and tenon joints together, then butt the blocks between the two sides of each post and the base, attaching them with glue and 25mm (1in) nails.

FINISHING THE BIRD HOUSE

Give the whole of the bird house several thorough applications of red cedar preservative, remembering to apply it inside the roof structure, so that none of the wood is left unprotected. This type of preservative not only gives the woodwork a pleasing red colour, but also adds an important water-repelling surface that will permit the finished bird house to withstand all weather, although it should be re-treated periodically.

CONSTRUCTING THE SUPPORTING POLE

The long supporting pole is made from a length of 45 × 45mm (1¾ × 1¾in) timber, with a cross attached at the bottom to provide a firm anchorage in the ground, and a similar but smaller version at the top, which fits into the underside of the base, between the battens. The length of the pole should ideally be no less than 2,100mm (82⅝in), with the provision for up to 600mm (23⅝in) being buried in the soil. If you think this will place the bird house beyond your reach, reduce the length slightly – but keep the top of the pole well clear of the ground otherwise you will certainly attract the attention of the neighbourhood's cats.

Make the cross for the base from two 600mm (23⅝in) lengths of timber, half-jointing them at the centre. Glue the joint together and, when dry, drill a

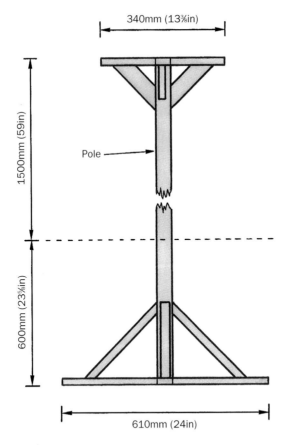

Side elevation of supporting pole.

The two arms of the small uppermost cross are half-jointed together.

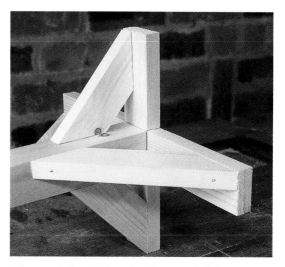

The cross is dowel-jointed to the top end of the supporting pole and strengthened with braces.

16mm- (⅝in-) diameter dowel hole in the middle of the joint and a corresponding hole in the end grain of the pole. Cut a length of dowelling and glue this into both the holes, tapping the cross tightly up against the pole. Now cut four 300mm (11⅞in) lengths of timber for the braces and prepare a mitre at each end, joining these between the base and the pole with glue and 38mm (1½in) nails. Once the glue has set hard, give the bottom 600mm (23⅜in) of the pole, together with the cross and the braces, at least two thorough coatings with cold bitumen to prevent the wood from rotting in the soil.

Prepare a smaller cross and braces at the top of the pole, noting that the two arms of the cross are unequal to one another, measuring an amount corresponding to the distances between the base battens. Make four short mitred braces to support the cross, these being purposely fitted off-centre to leave room for a single 6mm- (¼in-) diameter hole to be bored near the end of each of the cross's four arms, the holes being continued up through the base boards of the

bird house. Through these holes are passed the galvanized bolts that are secured with plain washers and a fixing nut.

Finishing Off

Apply several coats of red cedar preservative to the upper part of the pole, including the fixing cross, to the point where the cold bitumen leaves off. Now, it only remains to dig a large hole in the garden to receive the base of the pole. If you have decided to place the bird house in the middle of the lawn, it would be advisable to remove several surrounding portions of turf; these can be replaced later.

Check that the hole is deep enough to receive the desired depth of hole, and line up the pole against a spirit level before shovelling the soil back into the hole. Include a few rocks to give it a more solid foundation. The bird house is now ready to be stocked with bread crusts, bird seed and perhaps a bag of nuts.

CHAPTER 14

Patio Food Trolley

This food preparation trolley is a useful and attractive addition to the household, and although it may well spend quite a lot of its time in the kitchen, as it is fully mobile it can easily be taken into the conservatory and garden. Built entirely from oak, its main features are a convenient worktop, three storage drawers for utensils – which can be opened from either side – and a pull-out tray beneath. Four lengths of brass-coloured metal tubing prevent large items from sliding off the bottom shelf, and serve as handy towel rails.

DESIGN AND MATERIALS

As an alternative to oak, you could choose ash or beech; the lighter hardwoods are most suitable. But this brings us to the source of the material. If you have a joinery in your locality that specializes in making hardwood windows, doors and frames, it should already have a range of woods such as oak, ash or beech in stock, and if not, would be able to obtain them quite easily. But this trolley has wooden components that are wide, and the boards for the shelves and the tray need to be made up specially. Even the end panels and large drawer fronts are rather wide.

This is clearly an instance when you might benefit from breaking up an old unwanted piece of furniture such as a wardrobe, a sideboard, or even old solid bed-ends, salvaging as much as possible, and having wide sections of material planed to the required size by an obliging joinery. You could, of course, make up the boards yourself.

OPPOSITE: The finished patio food trolley in the conservatory.

MEASURING AND CUTTING

The Legs and Leg Joints
Start by cutting to length the four legs from 38 × 38mm (1½ × 1½in) material, allowing an extra 19mm (¾in) at the top for the tenon. Cut the two top end rails from 50 × 38mm (2 × 1½in) wood, again allowing extra length at each end so that the mortises can safely be cut without the risk of splitting the ends.

Mark in the position of the mortises on the underside of both rails to receive the leg tenons. The mortise gauge should be set to 13mm (½in) between the two spurs, and the fence adjusted so that they mark the wood centrally. Each mortise is then set in by 3mm (⅛in) from its inside edge and 9mm (⅜in) from the outside. Cut all four mortises to a depth of 19mm (¾in). It is best to remove the bulk of the waste by drilling out with a 9mm- (⅜in-) diameter auger bit, finishing with a 13mm (½in) chisel.

Mark out a corresponding tenon at the top of each leg, cut away the waste with the tenon saw, and carefully trim the four shoulders of each tenon until the joints fit perfectly.

The Top Side Rails and Shelf
Now cut the two top side rails from the same 50 × 38mm (2 × 1½in) material, once again giving an extra amount at each end to account for the tenon that will be prepared to fit into mortises cut in the top end rails. Taking the board for the top shelf, accurately measure its thickness – it should be 13mm (½in), but if you use veneered ply, it might be a fraction more – and set the pointers of the mortise gauge to this measurement. Adjust the fence to a gap of 6mm (¼in), and mark in

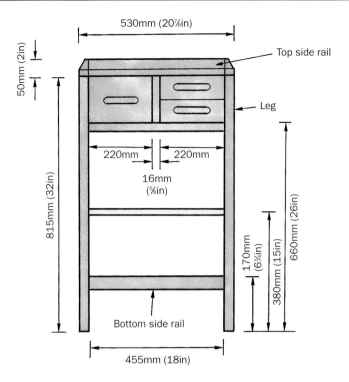

530mm (20⅞in)

50mm (2in)

Top side rail

Leg

220mm

220mm

16mm
(⅝in)

815mm (32in)

170mm
(6¾in)

380mm (15in)

660mm (26in)

Bottom side rail

455mm (18in)

Side elevation.

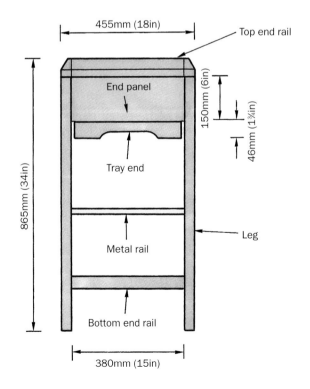

455mm (18in)

Top end rail

End panel

150mm (6in)

46mm (1¾in)

Tray end

865mm (34in)

Metal rail

Leg

Bottom end rail

380mm (15in)

End elevation.

the groove that runs along the inside face of each top rail, working the gauge from the uppermost edge. When cut, these four housing grooves accommodate the top shelf.

The grooves should be cut with an electric router fitted with a 13mm (½in) cutter, set to a depth of 9mm (⅜in). This is an occasion when the cutting of the grooves needs to be so precise that really the electric router is the only answer, although the plough plane is a possible alternative. However, the two top side rails have the grooves cut along their entire length, but the grooves in the two end rails are stopped 28mm (1⅛in) from each end. This is why the router, being more accurate to control for the preparation of a stopped groove, is the best tool for the job. You only then need to square off the rounded ends of the groove with a 13mm (½in) chisel.

The upper half of the outside faces of all four rails is chamfered, to give a sloped, decorative effect. The area of waste should be marked with the gauge: score a line halfway down the outside edge, running along the length of the material, and set a line in by one-third of the thickness along the top edge. Clamp each piece firmly in the vice and plane off the waste.

The two end rails are attached to the two side rails with mortise and tenon joints, the mortises being cut

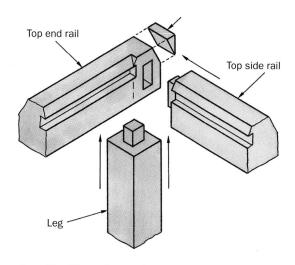

Assembly of leg and top rails.

in the end rails and the tenons in the sides. A depth of 9mm (⅜in) for each joint is desirable – any more than that, and there is the risk of cutting into and weakening the leg joints. If 9mm (⅜in) seems rather shallow, remember that these joints are further strengthened by the top shelf, which is dowel-jointed into its four grooves.

Trim the four joints so that the rails fit neatly

Patio Food Trolley Cutting List

Leg:	Four of 834 × 38 × 38mm (32⅞ × 1½ × 1½in)
Top side rail:	Two of 473 × 50 × 38mm (18⅝ × 2 × 1½in)
Top end rail:	Two of 455 × 50 × 38mm (17⅞ × 2 × 1½in)
End panel:	Two of 392 × 150 × 16mm (15⁷⁄₁₆ × 5⅞ × ⅝in)
Dividing panel:	One of 447 × 178 × 16mm (17⅝ × 7 × ⅝in)
Tray rail:	Two of 455 × 45 × 25mm (17⅞ × 1¾ × 1in)
Bottom side rail:	Two of 455 × 38 × 19mm (17⅞ × 1½ × ¾in)
Bottom end rail:	Two of 380 × 38 × 19mm (15 × 1½ × ¾in)
Large drawer front:	Two of 216 × 146 × 19mm (8½ × 5¾ × ¾in)
Small drawer front:	Four of 216 × 74 × 19mm (8½ × 2⅞ × ¾in)
Large drawer side:	Two of 417 × 146 × 13mm (16⅜ × 5¾ × ½in)
Small drawer side:	Four of 417 × 74 × 13mm (16⅜ × 2⅞ × ½in)
Drawer bottom:	Three of 424 × 196 × 6mm (16¹³⁄₁₆ × 7¾ × ¼in)
Tray end:	Two of 368 × 45 × 19mm (14½ × 1¾ × ¾in)
Tray side:	Two of 455 × 32 × 16mm (17⅞ × 1¼ × ⅝in)
Tray bottom:	One of 460 × 356 × 6mm (18⅛ × 14 × ¼in)
Top shelf:	One of 470 × 395 × 13mm (18½ × 15½ × ½in)
Bottom shelf:	One of 470 × 395 × 13mm (18½ × 15½ × ½in)
Long brass tubing:	Two of 473 × 19mm diameter (18⅝ × ¾in diameter)
Short brass tubing:	Two of 398 × 19mm diameter (15⅝ × ¾in diameter)

Cutting a groove with the electric router.

together to make a frame for the top shelf. Mark in the sloped contour of both the side rails against the two end rails, at the same time trimming the end rails to their final length, copying the sloped face of the chamfer in the process. This is quite a difficult procedure, and requires great care.

Next, lightly chamfer the inside top edges of all four rails, working the bevel along the full length of the side rails, and stopping it short on the end rails where it coincides with the chamfering of the side rails. The end rail chamfering is best done with a spokeshave, and cleaned up with a sharp chisel so the bevels meet perfectly at the rail joints.

Fitting the Top Shelf
Check that the top shelf material fits fully into its housing grooves, then measure it carefully to the correct size, taking the depth of the grooves into account, and cut it with the jigsaw, planing the edges smooth and square. Make a trial fitting to ensure that it fits fully into its grooves and that the four rails join perfectly to form the surrounding frame. For greater strength, the top shelf is dowel-jointed to the rails; drill a single dowel hole at the centre of each groove, and a corresponding hole dead centre in each of the top shelf's four edges; bore the holes with a 6mm (¼in) auger bit, drilling to a depth of 13mm (½in).

ASSEMBLING THE FRAME

Cut four 25mm (1in) lengths of 6mm- (¼in-) diameter dowelling, running a shallow glue channel along the length of each one with the tenon saw, and chamfering the ends with a pencil sharpener. Brush wood glue well into the dowel joints, the grooves and the mortise and tenon joints. Tap the assembly together, and cramp it firmly while the glue sets hard.

Fitting the End Panels
Fit the two top end panels to the legs with mortise and tenon joints (although these resemble housing joints). Each panel is 16mm (⅝in) thick, and mounted flush with the inside face of its two supporting legs. Each mortise is 6mm (¼in) wide, set up by 13mm (½in) from the bottom edge of the panel. The corresponding tenon is marked centrally along both ends of the panel. Cut out the mortises with the router, fitted with a 6mm (¼in) cutter set to a depth of 6mm (¼in). Stop the router at the point where the mortises end, and square off with the chisel.

Mark the tenons on the panels, using the same gauge setting, and remembering the 13mm (½in) haunch at the bottom. Cut the tenons with the saw, router, chisel, or a combination of all three, and test their fitting in the mortises. Drill a single 6mm (¼in)

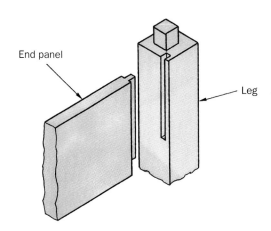

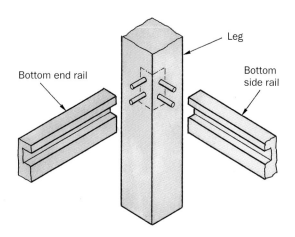

Leg to end panel mortise and tenon joint.

Leg to bottom rail dowel joints.

dowel hole in the exact centre of each panel, 13mm (½in) deep.

Fitting the Bottom Rails

Mark the positions of the 'brass' rails – 19mm (¾in) if you have 19mm- (¾in-) diameter tubing – in all four legs. This tube is not actually brass, but a bright-finished metal; you can use real brass, of course, if you prefer. Set the holes slightly off centre towards the inside edges, and drill them out to a depth of 13mm (½in) with a 19mm- (¾in-) diameter centre bit.

Mark in the position of the four bottom rails that are dowelled to the legs with two dowels at each end. Cut the four bottom rails somewhat oversize, and then mark in and cut the grooves for the bottom shelf in the same way as you did for the top rails – as wide as the shelf is thick, set 6mm (¼in) down from the top edge, and 9mm (⅜in) deep.

Cut the rails to their exact length, with perfectly square ends, and then mark and drill accurately for the dowel holes in each end; before you drill, make sure you have the positions marked precisely in the legs, too. A template the same shape and size as the rail end section would be useful here, to give the necessary accuracy between the bottom shelf rails and the legs. Cut and prepare sixteen dowels to a length of 25mm (1in) each, chamfering the ends, and glue them into the rail ends. Allow a day for the glue to set hard. Cut the brass tube to length, allowing for it to sit 9mm (⅜in) into each hole, and file each end flat.

Fitting the Castor Wheels and Tray Rails

Clamp each of the four legs vertically in the vice one at a time, bottom end uppermost, and drill a 9mm- (⅜in-) diameter hole into the centre of the end grain to a depth of 38mm (1½in). Fit the cylindrical sockets that house the castor wheels, tapping them down with the mallet until the serrated shoulder of each one grips the wood. Our trolley has a set of 75mm- (3in-) diameter gold-coloured spoked wheels fitted with rubber tyres.

Fitting a wheel socket in the bottom of a leg.

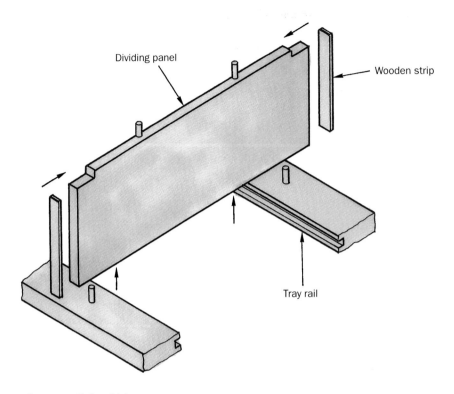

Centre dividing panel to tray-rail dowel joints.

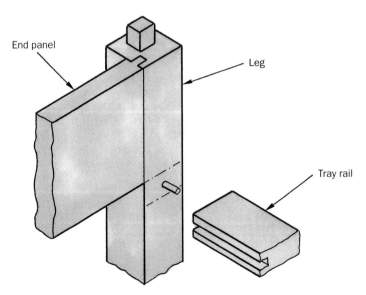

Leg to tray-rail dowel joint.

Mark in the position of the two tray rails on each leg, using another template, and drill a single 6mm-(¼in-) diameter dowel hole to a depth of 9mm (⅜in). Assemble the two ends, remembering to fit the 'brass' rails, gluing the joints together and cramping up.

FITTING THE TOP AND BOTTOM SHELF ASSEMBLIES

Cut the dividing panel that separates the drawers from one another to the same depth as the two end panels, notching it to fit around the top side rails and to butt up against the underside of the top shelf assembly. The ends of this dividing panel do not lie flush with the outer faces of the top side rails or the tray rails; they stop 4mm (⁵⁄₃₂in) short, leaving room to fit narrow strips of oak which cover the otherwise exposed end grain.

Drill two dowel holes of 6mm (¼in) diameter to join the dividing panel to the underside of the top shelf, and mark and drill the shelf as well. The divider is also dowel-jointed to the tray rails, so drill for these dowels now. Then glue two short dowels in place in the top edge and fit the panel in position under the shelf.

Uncramp the two end assemblies, and temporarily fit the leg tenons into their mortises in the top shelf frame assembly. This will give you the accurate length

for the two tray rails. Cut these rails from 45 × 25mm (1¾ × 1in) material, marking in a groove along the 25mm- (1in-) thick edge to receive the tongues of the tray. Scribe the positions of the grooves with the mortise gauge, its pointers set to a gap of 9mm (⅜in), the fence adjusted to place them centrally. Cut the grooves to a depth of 6mm (¼in) with the router, then trim both rails to the required length and drill dowel holes in their ends to match up exactly with the holes already marked and drilled in the legs. Drill for the dowels to match those in the under edge of the divider.

Trim the bottom shelf to fit into its rail grooves, cutting small notches in the corners for a complete fit.

Apply wood glue to all the joints, slot the bottom shelf into its housing grooves, place the metal tubing in its holes, and assemble all the dowel joints. Finally, join the four legs to the top shelf assembly, and cramp up tightly until the glue is dry. Upon removing the cramps, sandpaper the surfaces with medium and fine-grade paper.

MAKING AND ASSEMBLING THE DRAWERS

All three drawers are designed to be opened from both sides, and there is a built-in limiter preventing them from pulling right out, which simply consists of two

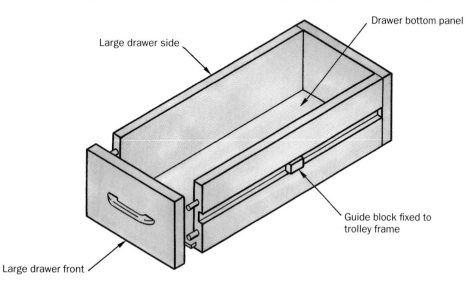

Large drawer assembly.

guide-blocks fixed to the frame along which each drawer runs. The drawer sides are grooved to accept the blocks. But the drawer fronts act as a stop to the grooves, so once they are assembled it is impossible to remove the drawers.

Cut all the drawer fronts to size, giving a clearance of 2mm (³⁄₃₂in) all around between their edges and the trolley frame. It is essential that, during assembly of the trolley, all the corners should be perfectly right-angled. Cut the drawer sides, matching each pair of sides to the same height as the drawer fronts. Run a groove along the outside face of each side, exactly halfway down, cutting these 19mm (³⁄₄in) wide and 4mm (³⁄₃₂in) deep using the router.

Also run a groove along the lower inside face of the sides to receive the drawer bottom panel, measuring 6mm (¹⁄₄in) wide and 4mm (³⁄₃₂in) deep. A corresponding groove is cut on the lower inside face of each drawer front, stopped 6mm (¹⁄₄in) from both ends.

The drawer fronts are assembled to the drawer sides with dowel joints; lapped dovetails may come to mind as an option, but they should not be used

here because it would be impossible to assemble the drawers properly – part of the assembly is carried out *in situ*.

Cut the drawer bottom panels from 6mm- (¹⁄₄in-) thick plywood, matching the colour as closely as possible to the oak.

Start by assembling the two sides to one drawer front, and add the bottom panel. When dry, fit this part-assembly into the trolley and accurately mark the position of the two grooves on to the frame. Cut the blocks of wood for the drawer guides and glue these in place halfway along the length of the end panels and the dividing panel, exactly on the line of the grooves in the drawer sides.

Slide the half-completed drawer into position on the guide blocks and fit the second drawer front. Add green baize to the bottom of each completed drawer, and fit drawer handles – six in all.

The tray is of similar construction, except that the sides have a tongue worked on their outside edges to slot into the grooves already cut in the tray rails. Both of the tray ends are given a curved bottom edge for decoration, and to form two feet upon which the tray

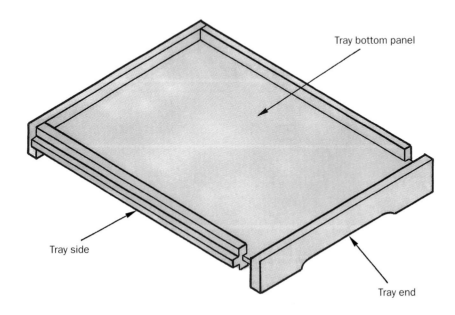

Tray bottom panel

Tray side

Tray end

Tray assembly.

The finished patio food trolley in the garden.

rests when it is taken out of the trolley and set down on a flat surface, giving room for the fingers of the hands to be withdrawn.

Grooves are cut for the tray bottom panel, and the sides dowel-jointed to the ends. Once assembled, the tray slides into its grooves and can be pulled out from either end.

FINISHING OFF

Finish the whole thing off with a semi-matt polyurethane varnish, which is hard-wearing and waterproof. Fit the four castor wheels into their sockets, and you have a practical and stylish piece of mobile house and garden equipment.

CHAPTER 15

Bench Seat

The garden bench seat has an ageless and charming character of its own, bestowed upon it by a traditional design, and a method of construction that depends entirely on the mortise and tenon joint to ensure maximum strength and solidity. With the right choice of timber and well cut joints, this seat will last for many years.

DESIGN AND MATERIALS

The first point to consider is what type of wood you should choose. For a project of this size, this is a rather difficult decision to make, because you have to balance the cost of the material against the quantity that is needed. The most desirable choice is unquestionably oak, a hardwood ideally suited by virtue of its extremely tough and durable nature; but oak is very expensive, and the amount required to build a large seat would certainly cost a lot of money, unless you can salvage the material from old oak timbers.

Otherwise the choice comes down to one of the cheaper imported varieties of hardwood known for their strength, attractive grain and the ability to withstand all types of weather. Iroko or utile will give good results; the seat illustrated is made from utile which, like sapele, is a reasonably good substitute for mahogany, possessing a finely structured grain with a pleasing reddish-brown colour. Iroko, on the other hand, resembles teak, and is a tougher material to work with.

The second point to consider is the size of the seat. You can decide for yourself whether your own garden seat should accommodate two, three or four persons. In terms of proportion, the best answer is the three-seater with an overall width of 1,524mm (60in), for this looks just right. However, you can alter the

The Garden Seat Cutting List

Front leg:	Two of 592 × 126 × 63mm (23¼ × 5 × 2½in)
Rear leg:	Two of 915 × 95 × 63mm (36 × 3¾ × 2½in)
Armrest:	Two of 546 × 63 × 63mm (21½ × 2½ × 2½in)
Side seat rail:	Two of 464 × 70 × 45mm (18¼ × 2¾ × 1¾in)
Mid seat rail:	One of 464 × 63 × 32mm (18¼ × 2½ × 1¼in)
Lower side rail:	Two of 464 × 63 × 32mm (18¼ × 2½ × 1¼in)
Upper backrest rail:	One of 1,480 × 70 × 45mm (58¼ × 2½ × 1¼in)
Lower backrest rail:	One of 1,480 × 70 × 45mm (58¼ × 2½ × 1¼in)
Front seat rail:	One of 1,480 × 95 × 45mm (58¼ × 3¾ × 1¼in)
Back seat rail:	One of 1,480 × 70 × 45mm (58¼ × 2½ × 1¼in)
Wide backrest slat:	Two of 305 × 120 × 22mm (12 × 4¾ × ⅞in)
Narrow backrest slat:	Twelve of 305 × 45 × 22mm (12 × 1¾ × ⅞in)
Seat slat:	Four of 1,480 × 63 × 32mm (58¼ × 2½ × 1¼in)

OPPOSITE: The finished bench seat.

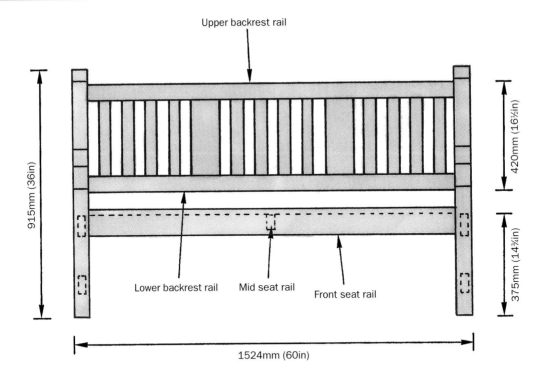

Front elevation.

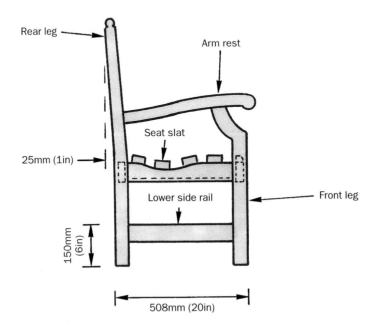

Side elevation.

dimensions to make the seat wider or narrower, according to preference, remembering that the wider the seat becomes – and therefore the greater its seating capacity – the larger must be the main components to bear the additional weight.

When viewed from the side, it is immediately evident that the seat has a number of curved or angled parts, and it is important to know how these shapes are obtained before launching yourself into the work, so that the correct amount of wood can be calculated and purchased.

The armrests and side seat rails are not curved to any great extent, and may be cut from the specified cutting-list sizes. The rear legs are raked back slightly, an angle being formed between the main part of the leg from the ground up to the seat, which is vertical, and the upper part that supports the backrest. This, too, is quite a straightforward piece of shaping work.

The front legs are given the most pronounced curve at the point where they join the armrest. It is wise to economize in this case by marking the two front legs in alternate directions on a single piece of timber that must be cut considerably longer than the actual length of each individual leg to allow for the curves.

From the side elevation it can be seen that the rake of the rear legs, the curve at the top of the front legs and the shaping of the armrest all contribute to give each end-frame of the seat a complicated configuration, in which the accuracy of the joints is of paramount importance. You will need to draw full-sized templates on large pieces of card so that the shapes and angles are reproduced exactly.

MEASURING AND CUTTING

Mark out all four templates on to thick card. A single large piece of card may be made up from several smaller pieces stuck together with sticky tape. Note that the rear leg is raked back at an angle so that the rear edge at the top lies 25mm (1in) further back than the lower vertical rear edge. The angle commences midway between the rear seat rail and the lower backrest rail, or a distance of 412mm (16¼in) from the ground. There is also a slight tapering at the upper end of the leg when viewed from the side, and a decorative

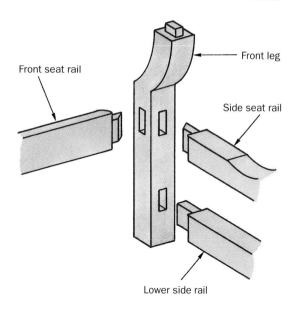

Exploded view of mortise and tenon joints for rails to front leg. The same arrangement is used to join them to the rear leg.

rounding effect at the top, with shallow shoulders cut in square.

The front leg, though shorter in length, is of a more complicated shape, with its inward-facing curve sweeping up to meet the lower edge of the armrest. Mark the curve on to the card with a pair of geometrical compasses, setting them to a radius of 190mm (7½in) for the outer curve, and 125mm (5in) for the inner.

The armrest, when viewed from the side, also has a rounded shape at the front end so that it comfortably receives the palm of the hand. There is a gentle concave dip along its upper surface with a corresponding curve worked along the lower surface to maintain a constant thickness of 50mm (2in) along most of its length, before deepening at the front end to a diameter of 60mm (2⅜in) or so.

Remember that a tenon must be cut: at the top of each front leg, where the curve straightens out; at the rear end of the armrest; and at each end of the side seat rail. Allow an extra 45mm (1¾in) of material for this purpose when cutting these pieces roughly to length. You will later have to trim some of this back to suit the size of the individual tenons, but for the moment it ensures that you have sufficient length available. There is nothing worse than underestimating the required length of a tenon, and finding that it is too short.

Cutting Out the Templates

Cut out the four templates with a sharp knife, laying them in place with respect to one another on a flat surface to check that they form an accurate pattern of the end frame. Note that the lower side rail is missing, but as this is a straight length of timber with no shaping, there is no need to make a template for it.

Mark around each template in pencil on the corresponding lengths of material. You will recall that the two front legs are marked on a single piece of timber for the sake of economy, with the curves placed at opposite ends in alternating positions. The best tool for cutting all the shaped pieces to size is the jigsaw, fitted with a coarse blade to cut quickly through the wood. If you have access to a bandsaw, so much the better. Alternatively, you can use a coping saw and achieve perfectly good results, but this will take you much longer. Whichever method you use, be sure to cut on the waste side of the pencil line, leaving a small amount to be trimmed by hand. Check that the blade of the saw is worked exactly at right angles to the surface of the wood, otherwise there will be the risk of serious undercutting.

Manipulate the saw gradually around all the curved sections, taking extreme care to avoid scorching the wood: this is particularly a danger with high-speed power saws, due to the heat generated by friction. Remove the remaining waste with a spokeshave. Its chief usefulness is being able to follow all the inside curves where an ordinary smoothing plane could never reach. As with any cutting instrument, the blade of the spokeshave must be kept very sharp, and adjusted to the optimum setting for the best result. Finish off by rubbing down with medium-grade sandpaper.

Marking and Cutting the Joints

The next step is to mark in and cut the mortise and tenon joints: for the main part of the seat frame, these are of the four-shouldered pegged variety. With the availability of strong, reliable, synthetic waterproof wood glues that are well suited to outdoor furniture joints, there is not the same need for the pegs – nevertheless they remain a desirable reinforcement and assist during assembly by the process known as 'draw-boring', where the joint is pulled tightly together as the pegs are driven into their holes.

All the mortises used for jointing the main components of the frame need to be as large as possible, to give maximum strength. It is usual to arrange for the mortise to equal one-third the thickness of the pieces

Marking out the front leg with the template.

Cutting the front leg to shape with the jigsaw.

to be joined together, but in this case some of the pieces are of different thickness. For example, all the rails are narrower than the legs; only the armrest is the same. This does not matter greatly, and the most appropriate width for the mortises is 19mm (¾in). This is only slightly less than one-third the thickness of the armrest and the legs, which are 63mm (2½in) thick, and more than one-third the thickness of the rails, which are 45mm (1¾in) and 32mm (1¼in) thick, depending on the rail.

Set the spurs of the mortise gauge to a gap of 19mm (¾in), and adjust the fence so that they mark at the centre of the legs. Now measure in the positions of the two side rails on both the front and rear legs, and mark them with a pencil and square. The length of the mortise is determined by the width of the rails, the side seat rails being 70mm (2¾in) wide, and the lower side rails 63mm (2½in) wide. However, the secondary pair of shoulders requires the mortise to be set in by 6mm (¼in) at each end so that when assembled, no part of the joint is visible.

Having set the limits of the mortises, scribe two parallel lines between the squared pencil markings with the spurs of the mortise gauge. Similarly, mark in the mortise positions for the long front and back seat rails and the backrest rails. The seat-rail mortises are

Shaping the curve of the front leg with the spokeshave.

each set at exactly the same height as the mortises for the side seat rail in both front and rear legs, and these are cut in such a way that the mortises meet within the wood.

The backrest mortises are slightly different, because the raked part of the rear leg has a tapered profile, so that the upper end is narrower than the lower part where the raked angle begins. This does not create any real problem, as it is simply a question of resetting the fence of the mortise gauge so that its two spurs mark centrally at the top of the leg, just below the rounded end grain. Use this same setting to scribe the mortise lines for both top and bottom backrest rails, working the gauge from the forward edge of the leg.

The quickest way of removing the waste from the mortise is to drill a series of holes along its length using an auger bit fractionally smaller in diameter than the width of the finished joint – a 16mm (⅝in) drill bit is best for this purpose. Mount it firmly in the handbrace, and place a depth-guide on the stem of the bit at a distance of 40mm (1⅝in) from the cutting tip. The depth-guide need be no more than a piece of sticky tape bound around the stem, so that you know when to stop drilling. If your workbench is equipped with a pillar drill fitted with its own graduated depth-guide, use this to bore out a series of holes along the marked-out area of the mortise, pausing often to clear out the accumulating scraps of wood.

Chop out the remaining waste with a 19mm (¾in) chisel and mallet, cutting to the required depth of 40mm (1⅝in), and working the chisel carefully to ensure that the sides and ends of the mortise are vertical. Where two adjoining mortises meet inside the wood, their sides should coincide at right angles, and the ends merge without any ridges between them.

Now for the rail tenons. Remember that there are two rail thicknesses – 45mm (1¾in) and 32mm (1¼in). Taking the seat and backrest rails first, begin by cutting all the long rails to length, squaring off at the shoulder positions with pencil lines. Having originally allowed at least 45mm (1¾in) for the tenons, trim these back to 40mm (1⅝in), giving an overall length of 1,480mm (58¼in) for the long rails, and 464mm (18¼in) for the side rails.

Adjust the mortise gauge fence to scribe its parallel lines centrally across the 45mm- (1¾in-) thick edge of the four long rails. The two backrest rails are both 70mm (2¾in) wide, and so is the rear seat rail, but the front seat rail is wider, at 95mm (3¾in). Mark in the tenons, then clamp each piece in the workbench vice and remove the waste with the tenon saw to form the two main shoulders. Next, mark in the secondary shoulders, setting in the wood by 6mm (¼in) each, and trim these also. However, because the front seat

rail is much wider than the length of its mortise, you must cut a deep third shoulder at the top before the joint will fit.

ASSEMBLING THE MAIN FRAME

At this stage it is not possible to assemble the long seat rails and side seat rails fully into their adjacent mortises at the same time, because each tenon blocks the full entry of its partner. The solution is to cut mitres at the end of each pair. Loosely assemble both end frames, consisting of the front and rear leg, the side seat rail and the lower side rail, and place the armrest in position according to its correct height. Because the rear end of the armrest joins the rear leg at a point where the leg is raked backwards, it is advisable to mount it at a slight angle so that it meets the rear leg perpendicularly.

Mark in the mortise on the back leg, and the tenon at the rear end of the armrest, cutting these to the same 40mm (1⅝in) depth, and make a trial fitting. Reassemble the end-frame components again, and with the armrest aligned accurately against the rear leg, mark a pencil line across the front leg to indicate the depth of the tenon, and pencil in the limits of the mortise. There will be a small amount of movement in this joint as it is the last one to be cut, so you are advised to set the length of the mortise to 50mm (2in) and no more, keeping it well inside the width of the front leg.

The mortise cannot be cut as deeply in the armrest as in the other members, and a depth of 32mm (1¼in) is recommended. Cut out both parts of the joint and fit the armrest in place to complete the end-frame assembly.

MAKING THE SEAT AND BACKREST

Before sawing the mid seat rail and backrest slats to length, it is advisable to check the temporarily assembled seat so that its frame can be seen to be standing square on flat ground with all joints fitting fully and accurately. Measure the distances between the front and back seat rails, and the top and bottom backrest rails. Note that the main part of the mid seat rail will need to be longer than both of the side seat rails, once you discount the tenon at each end, because the front and back seat rails are set back by 9mm (⅜in) from the inside edges of the front and rear legs. The total rail length is the same, but the mortises in the rails are not cut as deeply as those in the legs, so the tenons will themselves be shorter.

There is a further difference between the single mid-seat rail and its two side seat-rail partners. It is cut from a smaller cross-section of material, equal in size to that used for the lower side rails. However, you can use the same card template to mark in the dip, and the same method as for the previous curved surfaces, sawing away the bulk of the waste, shaping with the spokeshave and smoothing with sandpaper.

Dismantle the frame of the seat to separate the two long seat rails and the two backrest rails. The front and back seat rails are of differing widths, the front one being wider than the back so that its uppermost edge is aligned with that of the four seat slats. Measure the mid-point along the length of both rails to give the position of the mid seat rail.

When marking in the mortises at these mid-points, each one is set in by 9mm (⅜in) from the top and bottom edges. Note that the mid seat rail is not as wide as the two rails to which it is jointed, so it is set up from both bottom edges in order that the curved top edge be in alignment with that of the side seat rails. When you add this 6mm (¼in) difference to the setting in of the second pair of tenon shoulders by 9mm (⅜in), you will find that the lower end of each mortise is 16mm (⅝in) from the bottom edge of the rails in which it is cut, which is ample.

The width of the mortise and the thickness of its corresponding tenon is 19mm (¾in), as with all the other main joints. Mark in the two mortises using the pencil and square – the mortise gauge cannot be employed in this instance, although it should be used for the marking of the tenons.

Cut the joints in the usual way, and make a test fitting of the mid seat rail and the two long seat rails so that they form an H-shape.

Reassemble the two long seat rails to the end-frames of the seat, and check that the mid seat rail lies at the same height as the two side seat rails, with the curves in perfect alignment. This is best ascertained by laying one of the seat slats across all three rails. If, by some chance, the mid seat rail is found to be too high, you can trim the bottom cheek of the tenons to drop it slightly, packing the space above with thin strips cut from waste material. Conversely, if the rail is too low, trim the uppermost cheek and pack below.

Fitting the Backrest Slats
The next stage is to fit the slats between the top and bottom backrest rails. The total number used in the illustrated example is twelve narrow slats and two wide slats, arranged at regular intervals into the pattern four-one-four-one-four. If you wish, you could alter this to a pattern of your own choice, but you should bear in mind that it would be a mistake to economize on the number of slats by arranging them at wider intervals, because this will only result in the backrest appearing far too open.

To determine the exact distance between each of the slats, measure the width of one wide slat and multiply this by two, then measure the width of a narrow slat and multiply by twelve. Add these two amounts together to give the total width of all the slats, subtracting this from the length of the backrest rails minus their tenons, giving the overall space that will be left open. This figure, in millimetres or inches, must now be divided by fifteen – the number of gaps between all of the slats and the rear legs – leaving you with the width of each individual opening. Double-check the measurements to make sure that you are correct.

You will find it much easier to work in metric, since the increments are smaller, but if the resulting measurement is not an exact round figure but a fraction, you must take this into account in order to ensure that the gaps are all the same. But to safeguard against the possibility of compounding a small error with each measurement in moving from one end of the rails to the other, start from the centre and work outwards in both directions so that any tiny inaccuracy will only show in the two gaps occurring at the two furthermost ends, maintaining the basic symmetry.

Mark in a series of lines with the square and pencil along the lower edge of the top backrest rail, and the upper edge of the bottom backrest rail, to define the limits of the mortises that need to be cut, carefully checking the four-one-four-one-four configuration

The mortises cut in the top edge of the bottom backrest rail.

as you go along. Each slat being fitted in place between the two backrest rails with mortise and tenon joints, the mortises should all be marked to a width of 13mm (½in), their length being equal to the width of the relevant slat, minus a setting in of 6mm (¼in) at either end.

Set the spurs of the mortise gauge to the required gap of 13mm (½in), and adjust the fence so that the mortises are set 9mm (⅜in) back from the forward face of the two rails. Mark in each of the fourteen mortises for both rails, taking care not to scribe the lines accidentally over the gaps between the slats, confining them to the slat positions only.

Cut all the mortises to a depth of 13mm (½in), using the same technique all the way along both rails: start by drilling a series of holes with the 9mm- (⅜in-) diameter auger bit, then chop out the waste with the 13mm (½in) chisel. Measure and cut all the slats to length, marking in the tenon at each end, re-setting the fence of the mortise gauge so that the spurs scribe centrally across the 19mm (¾in) thickness of the slats. This will give shoulders 3mm (⅛in) deep. Because these are so shallow, you may find it easier to use the following method to prepare them.

Taking each slat in turn, clamp it flat on the workbench, or hold it firmly in the bench hook, and saw along the shoulder line to a depth of 3mm (⅛in) with the tenon saw. Then take the 13mm (½in) chisel and gently tap it along the scribed line on the end grain until the wood begins to split. Work the chisel carefully along the entire width of the slat, prising the waste away. Clean off any remaining waste with a paring action of the chisel to leave well defined shoulders.

Fit each slat into its appropriate mortise, trimming where necessary to achieve a perfect fit, and make a trial assembly of the two backrest rails once all fourteen slats are in place. Now fit the entire assembly to both end frames to check that the four main joints still line up accurately, allowing for the fact that the presence of the slats may now make a slight difference to the distance between the two backrest rails, either setting them closer or further apart than when they were originally assembled without the slats. If the joints fail to fit accurately, trim the tenons at each end of the two backrest rails until the whole backrest assembly slots fully and easily into position between the two end frames.

Preparing the Seat Slats

The next stage is to prepare the seat slats. These are first measured to the required length, and cut with the jigsaw to give a smooth end grain. Lay them in place across the temporarily assembled seat frame to check that they are equal to the full width of the seat. Mark the screw-hole positions at both ends of each slat so that they are located exactly halfway across the width of the slat, and also halfway across the thickness of the two seat rails. There is no need to screw the seat slats to the mid seat rail, because you will only succeed in placing a row of screws in a rather prominent part of the seat, where somebody will eventually sit upon them to their discomfort.

Drill the holes at the end of the slats with a No. 10 woodscrew bit. Do not attempt to countersink the top of each hole, because the screws used for assembly will be fitted with matching cup washers for neatness and added strength. Screw a mild steel 63mm (2½in) No. 10 woodscrew into each hole to cut the thread, until the tip of the screw just emerges on the under-surface of the slats.

Arrange all four slats on the seat, measuring them carefully to set them at equal distances from one another, and by the same distance from the front and back seat rails. This may need some calculation, as with the setting apart of the backrest slats, and in this case the distances are a little more difficult to measure due to the dip along the top edge of the three short seat rails.

When you have placed the slats in the required positions, give each screw one or two turns with a short screwdriver – a vital tool, as there is only limited space beneath the armrest – so that a small impression is left on both the rails. Identify each slat by making a pencil reference mark to distinguish them one from another, and dismantle the seat entirely.

Clamp the side seat rails in the vice, and drill out the marked hole positions with the same No. 10 drill bit to a depth of 32mm (1¼in). Take the front seat rail and chamfer the top edge to form a slope towards the front face. As a guide to how much you should chamfer, set the marking gauge to 9mm (⅜in), and scribe this along the upper front face. Plane down to this line, with the chamfer extending approximately two-thirds of the way back across the thickness of the top edge.

Rub down all the seat components with medium-grade sandpaper, paying particular attention to the curved surfaces so that all marks left by the spokeshave are completely erased to leave a perfectly smooth finish. Sandpaper all the edges – except for those where two joints meet – to round them off.

ASSEMBLING THE BENCH SEAT

The seat is assembled in stages, beginning with the two end frames, followed by the backrest assembly, then joining together the end frames with the four long rails, and finally mounting the seat slats. Before assembly can commence, however, there is one last step needed to complete the preparation of the main mortise and tenon joints: this is the process known as draw-boring.

Draw-Boring the Joints

To put it simply, all the joints that are formed between the four legs, two armrests and eight main rails are secured in place with small wooden pegs cut from hardwood dowelling. Most of the joints have two pegs each, but some of the smaller joints, such as those cut in the armrests and the lower side rails, have only one peg apiece. The term 'draw-boring' means that when the holes are drilled for the pegs in both the mortise and the tenon, instead of the drillings passing through in a continuous straight line, the hole in the tenon is deliberately set slightly out of line so that the peg, when it is driven into the joint, pulls the two parts tightly together.

Start by measuring and drilling all the holes that pass through the mortises. These are all marked on the outward-facing part of the legs and the armrests, and are set in by 9mm (⅜in) from the edge adjacent to the mortise. Where only one peg is to be used, this is placed centrally through the side of the mortise; for two pegs, these are set in by 13mm (½in) from the ends of the mortise.

Clamp each piece firmly to the workbench and drill vertically down through the mortise with a 6mm-(¼in-) diameter auger bit in such a way that the drill

Assembling the seat slats with brass screws and cup washers.

bit breaks through on one side of the mortise and crosses its width before boring further into the other side. The hole should be drilled to a total depth of 45mm (1¾in). Having completed the mortise holes, fit the appropriate tenon fully into position and pass a nail or some other suitable marking device – the bradawl will probably be too short to reach – down the hole to mark its centre on one cheek of the tenon.

Dismantle the joint again and adjust the centre of the tenon hole from the mark made by the nail so that it is 2mm (¹⁄₁₆in) nearer to the shoulder. Cut the wooden pegs from 6mm- (¼in-) diameter dowelling, preparing each peg to a length of 50mm (2in). Chamfer one end by giving a few twists in a pencil sharpener – without this, the peg will be unable to carry out its function.

Assembling the End Frames
Apply a waterproof PVA wood glue by brush to the mortise and tenon joints of all the component parts for one end frame, tapping the joints together with the mallet and a block of clean scrap wood. Glue the pegs, and drive them into their holes one by one, leaving 6mm (¼in) or so projecting clear of the surface. Wipe away any excess glue from around the joints with a damp rag, and place the assembly to one side for at least a day so that the glue has time to harden. After this period has elapsed, trim off the ends of the dowel pegs with a sharp chisel so that they are flush with the surrounding wood, and finish off with sandpaper. Assemble the second end frame likewise, checking that it makes a perfect match with the first end frame.

Assembling the Backrest
When both end frames are complete, proceed with the assembling of the backrest, gluing all the slats into place between the two rails. Knock the joints fully home, and check that they are all square. Glue the joints at one end of the two backrest rails, and assemble this end to its corresponding end frame, draw-boring the joints with their glued dowel pegs.

Joining the End Frames to the Seat Rails
Next, glue the mid seat rail into position between the front and back seat rails, then apply glue to the joints

at the same end of the two long rails as for the backrest rails, assembling to the same end frame. Finally, glue the joints for the second end frame, knock these into place, and add the pegs. When the glue has completely set, and all the pegs have been trimmed back flush with the frame, rub down the whole seat with medium- and fine-grade sandpaper to remove all traces of it from around the joints.

Before adding the four seat slats, give the seat frame two or three applications of wood finish, brushing or rubbing well into the grain. There are various shades available, and you should choose one that matches closely the natural colour of the wood. Apply the same finish to all surfaces of the seat slats, including the end grain.

Mounting the Seat Slats
After the treatment has dried, assemble the seat slats to the seat frame. It is best to remove the steel screws that were originally used to cut the thread, and replace them with 63mm (2½in) No. 10 brass screws and matching brass cup washers. Brass screws were not fitted at the outset because brass is a relatively soft alloy, and the slot of the screw will be easily damaged if the screwdriver meets any resistance in the first fitting of the screw. It will also shear more easily under heavy load.

FINISHING OFF

So now the garden seat is finished, and it only remains to add one or two words of advice. Even with a durable hardwood and a good water-resisting finish, it pays not to let the seat stand permanently on grass – for one thing, it will not do the grass much good. If you wish the seat to take its position on the lawn, place small pieces of paving stone beneath the legs. You could also add small steel or brass 'domes of silence' to the bottom end grain of each leg, thereby ensuring that the woodwork always stands clear of the ground.

Exposure to sun, wind and rain inevitably has the effect of weathering wood, no matter how well it is protected. Make a point of giving the seat an annual treatment with a wood finish to keep it looking at its best.

Index